ENERGY
HEALING

Heal Your Life with Chakra Healing, Reiki Healing,
Guided Imagery, and Guided Meditation

SARAH ROWLAND

Energy Healing

Heal Your Life with Chakra Healing, Reiki Healing, Guided Imagery, and Guided Meditation

Sarah Rowland

Table of Contents

INTRODUCTION

Congratulations on downloading your personal copy of *Energy Healing: Heal Your Life with Chakra Healing, Reiki Healing, Guided Imagery, and Guided Meditation*. Thank you for doing so.

In this day and age, we are all forced to work hard and run around to get things done. We no longer live in a world where we can exist at our own pace, and it does not look to improve anytime soon. That being the case, we need to find ways to slow down and realign ourselves with our inner purpose, so that we may live the best life possible. As we learn to live up to the purpose of our inner selves, we find that things fit into place, and energy flows much easier, making daily and long term goals much easier to meet.

The following chapters will discuss some of the ways to practice energy healing, and how it will positively affect your life. The subject of energy healing is very broad, but it is deeply rooted in Eastern culture. Recently, these practices have made their way into the Western world and can act in tandem with traditional Western medicine to cure what ails us.

There are many ways to improve our lives through energy healing, and this book will discuss the basis of these practices, and go more in depth with the concepts of meditation, Reiki, guided imagery and much more.

You will discover how important it is to align your daily life with your inner purpose and your spiritual well-being. Even if you can't change your job or circumstances, there are little things we can do every single day to become more aligned with our true self, and the more we tap into that, the better off we will be.

Here, you will also find guided meditation sessions to help you on your way to practicing energy healing every day.

There are plenty of books on this subject on the market, thanks again for choosing this one! Every effort was made to ensure it is full of as much useful information as possible. Please enjoy!

Chapter 1: What is Energy Healing?

The idea of energy healing is a very broad subject, as there are multiple methods that can be used to accomplish the same goal. The linked goal between all of these practices is to realign the body's natural energy fields in order to restore health and wellness. That too sounds pretty broad, so let's explore that for a minute by thinking about why we would need to do this in the first place.

What we know is that the body is made up of energy. The atoms and molecules that make us up can be pared down to sets of positive and negative particles that interact with each other. In nature, energy prefers to flow a certain way, and if anything is done to disturb that interaction, it creates a chain reaction wave that offsets energy elsewhere. Now, this can apply to one organ in the body, our entire beings, and the way that we interact with the world.

The idea of energy can be a tough concept to grasp, as it cannot be tangibly seen, at least not to the average person. Everything in the universe is simply the energy we talked about before. When broken down, there are only positive and negative charges. All living things, human and animal alike, have developed brains that sort out the waves of energy that are perceived in the environment and make sense of them.

Our five senses are available to sense energy waves, which are then computed in the brain to develop a sight, smell, taste, sound or feeling that will be associated with this energy. For example, sitting under a pine tree gives us the sense of branches and leaves, and the smell of pine.

Energy healing has been around for ages and is believed to  have originated somewhere in the Eastern region, in countries like India and Nepal. The idea that the universe is made up of energy was well known throughout the ancient cultures of every civilization, including Native Americans in the United States, half way across the world from India.

As civilization dragged on, people became less in-tune with this fact, often turning to pharmaceutical medications to soothe what ailed them, whether a physical problem like arthritis or an emotional issue like depression. As a whole, humans were more willing to go with the efforts of modern medicine, rather than realigning a somewhat intangible energy field that could solve all of their problems.

Sure, the idea of the world being created by an intangible energy may seem like hocus pocus, but then we must also consider the workings of one of the greatest minds in history, that of Albert Einstein. His famous theories were based on the fact that the universe is just energy, and there is a specific order to it. Everything is interconnected because ultimately, we are all a part of the same energy field.

 Even more recently, Dr. Wilhelm Reich discovered that imbalanced energy within the confines of the body caused disease and distress, and fixing the energy would cure the ailment. This is the direction we would like to discuss more, as physical and emotional ailments are at the center of our health and well-being.

Luckily, there are groups of practitioners in existence that are still knowledgeable about universal energy and how it affects the body. These are the people who are most in-tune with the body today. The good news is, these ideas are also backed by science.

For centuries, practitioners spoke of a 'third eye.' This invisible eye was something everyone had, and it was the connection between the body in the flesh and its spiritual being. In pictures, it is depicted as a literal eye located just above and between our eyes. While not clearly visible to the naked eye, it was thought to be the eye that saw the most and was responsible for our emotional response to the world. Myths tell of supernatural powers being activated as the third eye awakens. If activated, we are able to see the future, tap into the full potential of our intuition, and be a step ahead of our counterparts.

The third eye acts as a sixth sense, allowing us to see above and beyond, including into different realms and universes. Instead of detecting sights and smells, your third eye detects patterns across your life. It can show you patterns of how you react in certain situations, things you gravitate toward, positive and negative, and when listened to, can be a guiding force to set you in the right direction. For some people, tapping into their sixth sense gives them the ability to see auras or the physical manifestation of energy surrounding a person. A body will emit a glow of varying varieties of color, which can usually be related to their personality and mood. We all emit these auras, but only a select few can actually see them.

Modern science has mapped the brain and found that this third eye actually exists. It does not work like a typical eye, in fact, it is responsible for much more. The pineal gland, which is centered in the middle of the brain, and, if our skulls were see-through, would be seen right on the forehead, as the mystical third eye was once imagined.

While the tiny gland remains a mystery, it is responsible for releasing the hormone melatonin, which regulates your circadian sleep and wake rhythms. This hormone is key to overall function and vitality in life, and we literally cannot live without it. The full potential of this pea-sized gland still remains to be discovered, and we will anxiously await those results.

Lots of things can set off an energy imbalance, including stress from the environment, inner turmoil and even physical problems like the decline in health. The goal of any type of energy healing is to offset this energy imbalance where it lives so that the body and spirit may come back to center, where it functions at its best.

The practices that will be discussed in the following chapters are just a few of the many offshoots of practices that involve energy healing. It is important that you experiment will have any option you come across, as everyone is a little bit different, and one method may click with you more than another, depending on what your needs are. Pay attention to your energy and mood while doing any given practice to determine if carrying on is right for you.

Chapter 2: The Power and Benefits of Energy Healing

Consider the idea of electricity for a moment. We have found ways to harness energy in which it can be created almost instantaneously, travel miles and miles to your home to power all of our daily appliances, all in a matter of milliseconds. In the worst cases, lightning can strike from a thunder cloud a mile into the atmosphere and incinerate its target before it even knew what happened. Electricity is so powerful that it can be dangerous if not used carefully.

Luckily for us, humans hover at a much lower energy frequency, hardly even close to the capacity of pure energy. However, some people can harness and use more energy than others. Maybe you have noticed that a friend or co-worker is always energized and ready to go. Perhaps they are simply pulling in more energy from the universe than you, and have it to burn. You can learn to harness this energy by fixing your energy flow and tapping into your full potential.

Since the entire universe is made up of energy, there is nothing that can't be improved via energy healing. With proper care, your body can work to its fullest potential without ailment and disease. Your emotional state can improve, with less stress and more happiness overall. You can attract people that value you and bring joy to your life. You can be successful professionally and personally beyond your wildest dreams if you simply tap into the energy that is already inside of you.

In order to get these results, we must know where you are starting from. Imagine your body as multiple strings of Christmas lights. Even if you do not celebrate, you are likely well aware of the pitfalls of these brightly colored strings of light. Hundreds of tiny bulbs are strung together by tiny, fragile wires. Every string can be connected to another, to eventually light up the tree, the house, or whatever else needs some cheer.

As the fragile wires and bulbs age, they become brittle and are more likely to lose electrical connection and fail. The dimming of one bulb may not have an effect on the aesthetics of your Christmas tree, but that's also not how it works. The problem is, each of those light bulbs is connected and requires the light before it to work for them all to work. So, if one goes out, they all go out. The energy cannot flow properly, and the holiday festivities come to a sudden halt.

The energy in your body works the same way. Our bodies are made up of systems of nerves that flow through every tissue, every organ. If one connection is lost, the whole system of energy is thrown off, and the body cannot work properly. One of the most obvious physiological examples of this is carpal tunnel syndrome. This is usually caused by a pinched nerve under the shoulder blade that prevents the entire arm from working properly. Sufferers experience pain and tingling and can be debilitating. Many cases can be resolved with physical therapy that removes pressure off of the affected nerve to restore energy balance to the arm.

Most energy healing is done through light touch between one person and another. Usually, a trained professional, the healer, is at the center of the work, and the patient is on the receiving end of the energy. As energy is of a fluent nature, it is possible to transfer energy from one person to another, and this is the basis of the healing properties.

This transfer of energy is done in a quiet, relaxed environment, like when getting a massage. Most people who partake in this healing feel a deep sense of relaxation during and after the treatment. Reducing this stress brings about a great change in the body, as muscles and nerves relax, getting back to their normal, functional state.

Specific energy healing is done to focus on the endocrine glands as well. This system is responsible for releasing toxins from the body, and if energy is blocked around this area, the toxic matter is allowed to build up in the body, causing lethargy, illness, and disease. Moving energy to this area promotes proper function and flushes toxins properly from the body. As these toxins are removed naturally, the immune system improves as well. If this system was formerly trying to eliminate these toxins, making the body more susceptible to attack, illness is much more likely. Removing this burden from the immune system increases overall wellness.

Energy healing can also help with small ailments as it boosts the immune system. Head colds, arthritis, general pain and inflammation can all disappear when properly and frequently treated with energy healing. Fixing energy pathways can reduce headaches, as energy and proper blood flow is restored to the brain.

The power of energy healing is also an important tool in chronic and serious illness, like cancer treatment. Generally, traditional treatments like chemotherapy and radiation are very taxing procedures that actually harm the body. Heavy chemicals and radiation are meant to kill off the cancer cells, but end up harming healthy cells as well. The body loads more energy to restore the healthy cells and often leads to symptoms of fatigue, malaise muscle loss and much more. The body requires a higher intake of energy from food to maintain this rebuilding process, but often symptoms of nausea and decreased appetite from treatment prevent this from happening.

Energy healing can help transfer energy from the universe into that body to help out. Also, unblocking energy channels can help things flow more freely, making it easier for the body to recover. Energy healing, combined with a proper, nutrient-rich diet can help the body produce the energy it needs to fight and recover from the disease.

Perhaps the most important benefit of energy healing is restoring emotional balance. As we know, emotions are centered in the brain, and they are manifested as hormones are released in the brain. If hormone  balance is off even the slightest bit, it can cause us to become moody, depressed and anxious, among a host of other problems. If you have ever experienced this, whether, for a short time or a long duration, you know how great of an impact it has on your overall health and life. Feeling depressed sucks your energy, makes you feel achy and generally sluggish. You can't concentrate on tasks, and socializing with others feels like a chore. Feeling this way for long periods of time can affect your social ties, career and overall quality of life.

Using energy healing to unblock energy channels that affect hormone balance is a great remedy to try. The feeling of relaxation and revitalization that accompanies an energy healing session may be all you need to get your hormones back in balance, and to start feeling well again.

The power of energy healing is actually boundless. Regularly partaking in energy healing sessions can improve health and emotional wellness across the board, leading to a better quality of life overall. Finding help from a practiced healer is your best bet, but it is possible to practice energy healing on yourself as well. More on that in the following chapters.

Chapter 3: Cleansing Your Energy

By now, you understand the powerful benefits of cleansing your energy through energy healing, but how do we go about doing this? If you are not ready to commit to meeting with an energy healer and getting on track that way, there are a multitude of simple things you can do at home to try and balance your energy on your own.

One of the strongest ways to accomplish this is through meditation. Like energy healing, meditation is nothing new, and you have probably come across this concept before if you are not already practicing. The concept is very simple. We must relax and focus our mind for the rest of our body, and our lives, to function properly. Our mind controls everything else, and so we must start here in our journey to overall wellness.

Meditation often calls upon energy from the earth to be imparted to the body to provide focus and insight. This energy surges throughout the body, pushing through energy blocks, resituating the mind where it should be. While there are many different types of meditation, asking for energy to enter your body is a great place to start.

Many offshoots of meditation offer benefit through passive means. That is, the mind has the ability to gather itself and focus by thinking of nothing at all. In fact, if your mind tends to wander, worry and get overwhelmed, there is a lot of benefit from meditating this way. Of course, as it does, energy will naturally flow in and out of you to create equilibrium with the environment around you. This process alone often leaves you feeling mentally acute and ready to handle the next task.

Energy healing takes meditation a step further. In this case, we do not passively meditate, hoping the universe will send us what we need. Instead, the idea of asking is imparted. In this asking, we sit  silently, and simply imagine the energy we require entering our body. Many practitioners imagine it coming in through the very top of their head, traveling down the spine, and hitting every nerve on the way through. Imagine the feeling of energy flowing down every limb, descending to every finger and toe. Ask and you shall receive.

Energy Healing

If meditation interests you, it is easy to get started. You will simply need a quiet room and yourself. Sit or lie down comfortably and focus on deep breathing. Let your breath steady and focus your mind on the ins and outs of your breathing. Let the stress of the day go and keep your focus. Once you have relaxed yourself a bit, decide how you would like to proceed. If you feel that honing in on your breath is energizing and fulfilling, keep that up. If you would like a little more, try asking for energy as the next step.

Practicing meditation daily, for about fifteen minutes can have amazing effects on your body and mind. If this is something you feel like adding to your daily routine, the last two chapters in this book are dedicated to guided meditation practice.

If meditation isn't in the cards, or you are looking for other simple things to do at home, look no further. There is a host of small, seemingly insignificant things that can be done on a regular basis to promote energy balance.

The first may seem obvious, you may not have realized its purpose. Most of us have partaken in a bath using bath salts. They are a popular Mother's Day gift as moms are usually characterized as stressed out. Salts are often infused with lavender and other essential oils to promote relaxation, but the salt by itself has amazing healing properties.

Salt is a polarizing substance. It draws water to itself. In the medical field, we are familiar with reducing salt to decrease fluid buildup that raises blood pressure and causes swelling, usually in the lower extremities. Water is a universal solvent, and everything, including toxins in the body, can be dissolved in this water. The salt draws this water out, toxins and all.

Salt is purifying in any form, and if you feel you don't have time for a daily salt bath, using it in the shower is another great  way to incorporate it. Have a small container of bath salt or regular sea salt in the shower. As you wash away, take a little of the salt and run it over your skin. As you do, imagine negative energy and toxins leaving your body, as they are. Touching the salts to your chakra points has an even bigger benefit. More on chakras in the following chapters.

As discussed earlier, the mind has the power over everything else in the body. In that effort, we must do everything in our power to keep our mind calm and relaxed, so that it may move the body in a similar way. One great thing to do is to keep the spaces in which we live and work organized, clean and in good working order.

If you struggle to find things at home, making daily tasks just a little harder, you are unnecessarily stressing your brain. If your home is cluttered and your eye cannot pick a pleasant focal point, you are stressing your brain. By cleaning and streamlining your home or office space, you relax the brain and make it easier to do daily things, saving that extra energy for healing, or to increase your productivity.

 We have discussed many ways to gain extra energy from the earth, but often, this can actually be detrimental. For anyone who is anxious on a regular basis, getting more energy may actually be a problem. When the mind is on edge and anxious, there is likely too much energy, usually negative, flowing through the body. Anxious people often fidget and pace in an effort to burn some of that negative energy off. Using techniques like meditation, we can release negative energy from the body as well. Instead of asking for it, we can ask to release it through the soles of our feet.

If meditation isn't possible at any given moment, taking a few seconds to imagine that energy flowing out of us in moments of panic can have similar results. Tell the earth that this energy is too much to bear, and ask it to take it back. Imagine it flowing right out of you, releasing your muscle tension and reducing your jitters.

Exercise is another great way to relieve this negative energy. As anxious people often fidget, it shows that they are trying to burn the energy off naturally. Doing physical activity has the same effect. Walking, running or jogging creates a great release of energy from the whole body. Other exercises, like yoga and stretching, also promote the unblocking of energy channels, which can help release energy naturally as well.

Naturally, everybody is a little bit different and will require a different way to unwind and re-energize themselves. Often, different techniques can be used at different junctures in life to produce a good energy balance. Energies change, ebb and flow, and so we must use different tactics to resolve it. Most importantly, we must listen carefully to what our bodies are telling us, and give energy to areas that are lacking, and remove energy from areas that are overstimulated. Continue with techniques that bring you peace and energy, and forgo those that do not.

Chapter 4: Awakening Your Higher Self

There is one topic we must discuss in order for everything else to make sense, and that is the idea of a higher self. We touched for a moment on this in Chapter 1, with the idea of our third eye, or our sixth sense. Let's explore this a little bit further.

The higher self is innate in every living thing. It has been called many things, including gut feelings and intuition, our soul, our spirit. To the untrained person, the higher self is an intangible thing. We cannot necessarily see it, hear it or physically feel it, but it is still there. When you have an inkling that something isn't quite right, or if you make a decision based on a gut feeling that may have no other logic, this is your higher self, guiding you in the right direction.

The good news is, we can be trained to become more in touch with our higher self. In fact, when we really look at it, our higher self is tangible after all. We can feel it, sense it, but only if we try. Imagine that this higher self is simply a small ball of energy that lives within us. For many spiritual followers, we know that our spiritual being will eventually leave our bodies in death, and leave to other parts of the universe. No matter

what religion you follow, if any at all, this idea transcends all. Religion is based on this idea, and we see it playing out in varying degrees of heaven, and places in which our spirit will be free from the flesh. We cannot simply imagine that our consciousness will not go on once our bodies have expired.

This ball of energy, our higher self, has a mind all its own. It is our guiding energy that knows right from wrong and knows our true path. Think for a moment about the state of your life. Think about your career, your family, how you choose to live your life. Are you content with everything, or are there other things that you strive for? Do you feel you are in line with your conscience, or is there a nagging feeling in the back of your mind that is pulling you in a different direction?

This feeling is with everyone, and there is nothing wrong with following it, as it is simply your higher self, trying to tell you something. Our society has fallen far from a once virtuous place in which everyone followed their inner voices and did what was best for them, for their communities and the earth they call home. Instead, the world is filled with greed, money, and the pursuit of a 'stable' life filled with inanimate objects like fancy homes and cars that bring 'happiness.' In reality, we do not need any of those things to survive, and listening to your true self will help you distinguish what is necessary and what is greedy.

Many of us try and push these feelings away, as society is telling us what we need. Our desire to follow the crowd and do what is socially acceptable has imprisoned our spirits into endless days of work and responsibility that is slowly killing our energy. We often push our desires down to go to a tireless yet well-paying job to make money and live a responsible life, all the while reducing our higher self to nothing.

Instead, if we learn to work with our higher self, we unlock the potential of endless bounds of energy, happiness, and life. Our higher self, that little ball of energy within us, holds the key to a fulfilling life, one that may not be so prosperous monetarily, but one that is worth living in the end. If we learn to follow our intuitions given by the higher self, everything we truly need will come to us when we need it.

Now for some training to get in line with our true self. Simply, we must learn to follow our gut instinct. Those little feelings of dread and cues for you to do certain things are your roadmap. Understand that stress, anxiety, and depression are symptoms of an unhappy inner self. Your energy is off balance, and something in your life is causing it. Instead of suppressing these feelings by medicating with sedatives and mood stabilizers or self-medicating with alcohol or other substances, embrace and explore these feelings. Something in your life isn't quite right, and finding out what it is and making changes is the key to balancing your energy and emotion. If you don't feel right, something is wrong. It is as simple as that.

We certainly would not recommend getting up and leaving your job and abandoning your current life, unless of course, this is the only way to find spiritual peace. Instead, take some time to really discover what your true path is by paying attention to those gut feelings and determining where it is they are telling you to go. You cannot expect to be good at being in-tune with your higher self immediately, so don't make any rash decisions until you become comfortable with its signals.

For example, if you have begun to dread going to work every day, it may not be because of the work, but because of the specific environment. You may enjoy that same work somewhere else and does not require a complete upheaval of your life. Maybe you just need to find work with another company to bring your balance back. Or, maybe you discover after switching jobs that your work is no longer fulfilling and finding something new is really what you need. Now may be the time to start looking into a new career, your true calling.

 Remember that the universe will give you exactly what you need if you stop working on its energy. Everyone has a true path that they need to follow, one that brings ultimate happiness and joy. Once you are in line with this ideal energy path, everything will fall into place on its own. Going against this energy is like trying to swim up river after a heavy rain. You will fight the current but get nowhere. Giving in and flowing with the river will get you where you need to be faster. You simply need to accept that this river of energy knows where it is you need to be.

If you are someone that needs something to 'do,' trying keeping a journal expressing your feelings and emotions in relation to your situation. You can quickly develop feeling patterns in relation to specific events, like work, with certain people that take advantage of you, or even your location. Maybe you do better living in the country in the peace and quiet that on city streets. All of these things are valuable pieces of information that will be necessary for plotting out potential life changes.

If this doesn't sound like you, know that your inner self will give you the wisdom and energy you need to navigate this life, and it will guide you as it sees fit. This doesn't require careful planning, just the ability to tap into your true feelings and emotions at any given time. This doesn't mean that you won't make mistakes. You need to experience certain things to gain knowledge and wisdom to make the next step. You are not necessarily on the wrong path, and as long as you feel in-line with your true self, there is nothing to worry about.

Chapter 5: Know Your Chakras

In order to complete true energy healing, we must understand our chakras. The chakra system developed in India thousands of years ago. The idea is that the body has seven chakras or discs of energy centered along the spine. In true symmetrical fashion, the chakras align with the spine, and their energy resonates to the rest of the body with the order.

Think of your spine and the center line of your body as a power cord. This cord receives energy from a 'plug' or in this case, from the universe outside. Energy flows from the head, down the spinal cord, and is then dispersed throughout the body. Each chakra is responsible for propelling energy onward and outward, and if one chakra is not functioning properly, the order of the entire system will be thrown off. This can occur during times of stress, making it even more important to remain calm and practice meditation and other methods to reduce stress.

Each chakra is responsible for certain things within the body. The first is our root chakra, which makes us feel stable and grounded to the earth. It is located at the lowest point of the spine, the tailbone. This makes sense, as if we sit to meditate, this is the point closest to the earth. In life, this chakra is responsible for feelings of security, both tangibly and emotionally. It gives us financial stability and emotional balance. When we are having problems with money, food security, and stability, it is often the root chakra that is out of balance.

Physically, it is related to our core makeup, our bones, our legs and our feet, that connect with the earth. Interestingly,  it is also related to our natural fight or flight response as well. When out of balance, we may feel paranoid and on edge, as our sense of security is failing.

The sacral chakra, located just above the root chakra on our sacrum allows us to connect with others, and to embrace new experiences and interactions with others. We will find this chakra just below our navel. Our feelings of general well-being and connection with our social circles originate here. This chakra allows us to be connected with another sexually as well. It is the center of procreation and has a hand in the circulatory system, kidneys and bladder. Physical symptoms like decreased kidney function or poor blood circulation may be a result of a blocked sacral chakra.

The third chakra is located on our solar plexus, or the area above the navel, the upper abdomen. As this is near the center of our body, it makes sense that this is where our feelings of self-esteem and worthiness come from. When this chakra is out of whack, we begin to feel worthless and get down on ourselves for formerly meaningless things. When back in alignment, we feel confident and in control of our lives. It is at the center of all emotions and physically can carry a big burden. This chakra is related to the gastrointestinal tract, pancreas, liver, and muscles, among other things. Chronic stomach issues or blocked pancreas and liver can lead to serious illness, making it very important that you have this chakra in balance. Emotionally, chronic feelings of anger, or that you are a victim in your daily life may stem from here.

The fourth chakra is very important and is located along the spine just above the heart. Not surprisingly, this chakra is responsible for our ability to love and embrace others. It is the center of inner peace and contentment. When feels of being unsettled and unable to trust others develop, it may be due to this fourth chakra. The absence of compassion or empathy is directly related to this area. It may also manifest itself physically with heart and lung problems.

The chakra found in the throat is the fifth of seven. As expected, this chakra is handy when it comes to communication. Our ability to conversate and get points across with others can either be helped or hindered by the functioning of this chakra. If you feel that others are not understanding you when you speak, it may be that you are not communicating clearly, and it is time to focus on this chakra. A block in number five can lead to a deficit in creativity and inability to think outside of our normal confines. This area is where our thyroid gland is located as well. Chronic issues with hypothyroid could mean chronic issues with your fifth chakra.

Moving up to the head, our sixth chakra is our sixth sense, or our third eye chakra. As we talked about before, our third eye is the strongest connection between our physical bodies and our inner selves. This chakra allows us to make sense of the world around us and analyze the small comings and goings of life in terms of the big picture. It gives us a sense of direction and allows us to make decisions and have the wisdom to do so. When this chakra is out of whack, you may be blindsided with problems that you never saw coming. Without your intuition, you may make decisions without true insight, and the consequences of your actions cannot be seen until they happen. When this chakra is in line, you can see the possible outcome of your actions ahead of time, prompting you to make an educated decision.

Our seventh chakra is the crown chakra and is the biggest connection to our spirituality. When in good order, we can be fully connected with our true self, allowing us to flow with the proper energy, and allowing us to find our true happiness. When out of line, we will find ourselves swimming against the current, against our true path. An imbalance can manifest itself through psychological symptoms, like depression, anxiety or more complex problems. Medically speaking, it is connected with the nervous system, which may manifest with pinched nerves, and tingling in the extremities. It also affects the pituitary gland, which plays a role in hormone production.

At any given time, any of these chakras can be in disrepair. Perhaps you have connected very specifically with one chakra while reading this. Maybe one of these struck a nerve, bringing some sense to some symptoms you have been experiencing. For example, if you have been experiencing money problems and low self-esteem because of it, your root and solar plexus chakras may not be aligned. Bringing proper energy flow back to these chakras could bring clarity to your financial situation, and instilling confidence in yourself to alleviate the situation.

Chapter 6: Heal Chakras and Realign Your Entire Chakra System

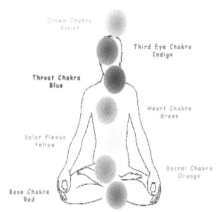

Now that we have connected physical and emotional problems to our specific chakras, it is time to get them back in alignment, so that our body and mind may function properly together. Perhaps you relate to symptoms of the imbalance of one or two specific chakras. While it may be necessary to focus energy on these to realign yourself, we must not forget to look at the big picture. Focusing energy on one chakra inadvertently removes energy from others. We must look at the system as a whole, making sure that every chakra is in the balance, so that we can live a fulfilling, happy life.

Let us start by working on each individual chakra. First, the root, number one. As we discussed, this is the chakra that makes us feel grounded and secure in life. When out of balance, we may have issues with money, we may feel a bit paranoid and unsure of our standing. This chakra is associated with the color red, so, therefore, we may strengthen this chakra with more exposure. It can help to surround ourselves with red things, but it may be more appropriate to eat foods that are red, rather than repainting an entire room.

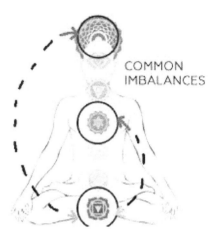

COMMON IMBALANCES

Eat foods that are deep red, like red meat, apples, beets, and red peppers. The color red is also associated with heat and warmth, so foods that are spicy, like hot peppers (red ones), can be beneficial as well. As this is the chakra of grounding, eating foods that come from the ground, like carrots and potatoes, so called 'root vegetables' are beneficial as well.

Certain yoga poses, like the bridge, which stretch muscles and tendons in this area can help move energy around in this area, stimulating the chakra. The action of simply walking barefoot on the earth may help as well. As the idea is grounding, it makes sense to get as close to the earth as possible to accept some new energy.

The second chakra, the sacral, is primarily responsible for connection with others, sexuality, and well-being. It may manifest itself as infertility, low sexual drive, and inability to fully connect with loved ones. Again, we can use food to help heal the chakra. Orange is the associated color, so orange peppers, carrots, and pumpkin are great foods to include.

In yoga, doing exercises like the cobra pose, or pelvic movements can help stretch and unblock energy channels in this area. Any stretches or movements that engage the pelvic area, including belly dancing, can help stimulate sex drive and increase fertility.

The solar plexus chakra is in the upper abdomen, so it would make sense that any movement involving this area would be beneficial. When this chakra is out of alignment, we may feel out of control of our life, and confidence wanes. Doing sit ups and other exercises that engage the core are beneficial. In yoga, doing poses like the boat pose engage the core, or dancing and shaking the hips engages the core as well.

The solar plexus is associated with the color yellow, and so foods that are yellow may help engage the chakra as well. Add lemon to water, and enjoy corn on the cob in the summer. Grains are also beneficial, as well as herbal teas like mint.

The heart chakra must constantly be nourished. Without it, we are not able to love or feel compassion for others. Physically, we may have heart trouble or problems with breathing. Reconnecting to this chakra will be very beneficial to our entire life. The only way to exercise our heart is to use it. In the physical sense, doing cardiovascular exercises like walking or jogging work the heart and lungs. In an emotional sense, we must practice loving and accepting others whole heartedly to exercise our chakra.

While you would expect its associated color to be red, it is actually green. Surrounding yourself with greenery in nature, and eating greens on the regular are great ways to engage your heart chakra. Ever notice how a hike in the woods really enhances your spirit? The combination of exercise and lush green environment stimulate your heart chakra. Eat a big salad and sip on some green tea after a long walk to get your heart in the right place.

The throat chakra is responsible for effective communication, first and foremost. It also holds the key to the thyroid gland, which makes hormones responsible for energy levels and much more. Imbalances lead to deficits in the thyroid gland, leaving you sluggish and listless. In this state, it will be much more difficult to communicate effectively.

The throat chakra is blue, so eating foods that are rich and blue, like blueberries are your best bet, although any fruit will do. Medically speaking, a person with underactive thyroid should avoid dark green foods, as their properties actually inhibit the thyroid. Do not avoid them altogether, as this can then throw off your heart chakra. Balance is the key here. Exercises that work the shoulders and arms are good for this chakra as well. Doing pushups during a workout and stretching your shoulders out across your chest as you cool down is very stimulating.

Since our third eye chakra provides a deep connection with our spiritual being, we must exercise and connect with it regularly. As it is located between our eyes, there aren't too many traditional exercises that reach this area. Eye motions, like eye rolls (not at your spouse), can work the area, and yoga poses like child's pose that places the forehead on the floor can stimulate it. Connecting with it on a daily basis by listening to cues given by your inner self is helpful as well. The third eye is indigo, and eating purplish blue foods like dark berries are beneficial. Your third eye also likes chocolate and lavender, which explains the need for both during stressful situations.

Finally, our crown chakra, responsible for our greatest spiritual connection, must be fostered. Located at the top of our head, we must get creative to exercise it properly. If you aren't feeling quite right, and are just unable to feel happy, spend some time nurturing the crown chakra. As this is very much mind-related, we must practice meditation and mindfulness to exercise this chakra. It is associated with the color violet, but eating a plethora of violet foods, which there are not many of, isn't overly beneficial. Focus more on your body-spirit connection to keep this chakra healthy.

You will have noticed that aligning all of these chakras has three main components. These are food, which provides

energy, exercise, with expends energy, and mind, which balances energy are all required. It only makes sense then, to exercise a host of these three components on a daily basis to maintain a powerful chakra system.

You will have noticed that

all of the foods mentioned were of good quality and nutrition. We discussed vegetables, fruits, meats, and herbs. No junk food, soda or fast food. This is not by accident. By incorporating foods that come right from the earth, our natural habitat, we are promoting good health of all chakras. Get a wide variety of fruits and veggies of different colors to receive different types of nutrients and energies that the body needs. Combine that with simple proteins from meats, nuts, and seeds for muscle maintenance and proteins that help make up the brain. Dietary fat is important as well, especially oils from olives, avocado, and fish, as the Omega 3 fatty acids within the help support optimal brain function.

A combination of different exercises is important as well. For good health, we must combine moderate intensity exercise like jogging and hiking to promote the heart, circulatory system, and respiratory system. We must also pair this with meaningful stretching to release tension from muscles and target the core and shoulders. Yoga and simple stretching after cardio can help us accomplish this. Remember that our physical body is where our spirit lives. It would be wise to treat it with the utmost respect and care while we are still here.

That said, we must also exercise our mind, mainly for our third eye and crown chakras. As both are centered on the head, the house for our brain, we must remember to use our brains to think logically and tap into the wants and needs of our inner spirit. Ignoring these signals causes our brain to fall into disrepair, and over stresses it. Paying attention to the proper signals leads us to better decision making, and allows us to flow with our natural course of energy.

If you feel that a certain chakra needs attention based on the current course of your life, or if you feel like you need to enhance certain aspects of your life, go ahead and focus some attention on one. Just don't forget that the entire system is connected and neglecting the rest for the sake of one chakra will only bring bigger problems. Do your due diligence to look at the big picture and live a life in balance with your chakra system.

Chapter 7: What is Reiki?

The practice of Reiki is of Japanese origin. The name is a combination of two Japanese words, Rei and Ki. While the translation can become a bit complicated, Rei is loosely related to the knowledge and energy that flows through everything. It is omniscient and knows all. It is often related to the idea of God in many religions. Ki, in simple terms, is the life force that rules the universe. When this Ki is high, we feel energetic and happy, and when it is low, we feel drained and ill.

The practice of Reiki harnesses the capabilities of both the Rei and Ki energy for healing. To practice Reiki, there must be a receiver and a practitioner. The receiver is the person in need of healing, whether it be a physical ailment, chronic disease or emotional state. The practitioner is in charge of focusing the energy of the universe into the receiver so that they may heal themselves.

A Reiki session is very relaxed and soothing. The practitioner takes their time, slowly connecting the palms of their hands with various points, usually in relation to chakras, on your body. This is not like a massage, as muscles are not being rubbed. The idea is simply to transfer energy from the practitioner to the receiver. This is done by simply holding the hands on the touch-point for a moderate length of time, before moving on to another point.

A practitioner does not hold the energy, only has the ability to draw it to the receiving person. Once a part of this person's energy field, it will go where it is needed most, at the site of the ailment. It is Ki that naturally energizes all vital organs, tissues, and cells. Without it, we develop serious illness and dysfunction within the body. Drawing in Ki from outside the body helps set the balance back in motion so that the body may do what it is supposed to do.

Unlike traditional Western medicine, this type of energy healing can do no harm, as the power to yield results is with the power of the universe. In modern medicine, fate is given to the hands of people, who often make mistakes. They give medications that do more harm than good. They carry out procedures that break the rules of nature. All in hopes of doing good, but actually disrupts the natural energy flow in the body, among many other things.

There is great control in the energy given by the universe. In fact, a person who is unwilling or skeptical about the practice rarely reaps the benefits. Positive energy from the universe can be upset by negative thoughts and emotions running through the body. Before getting started with any Reiki session, it is important to enter a relaxed state through meditation, so that energy will be allowed to flow freely throughout the body.

What is worse, it is this negative energy that is the likely cause of physical and emotional problems in the first place, making it extremely important to get our negative thoughts under control. The energy we are made up of is not contained within just the confines of our body. We actually have an energy field called an aura surrounding our bodies. We emanate energy.

Certain people are very tapped into energy fields, and can actually recognize auras around themselves and others. Auras appear as light, often colored, which reflects the current emotional state of the person. Calm, relaxed blues and greens signify calm, while reds may denote anger in the aura. The color and strength of the aura can change at any given time based on your emotional and physical well-being.

Auras are not one solid color or strength, it will vary. Think of it like the earth's ozone layer. Where the sun beats through, the ozone layer is thin, letting in more damaging solar rays. If your aura is thin in a specific area, there will likely be something physically wrong underneath. For example, if your aura is thin and red over your kidney region, it means that energy is restricted in this area and your kidney function could decline. Working on the aura in this region, as well as your chakra system will help bring energy back to the area, where it needs it most.

As medical procedures become more common, we must ask ourselves what is really right for our bodies. Is it best to suppress symptoms of physical and mental ailments with medications and procedures, or is it better to unmask the problem behind the symptoms that will ultimately lead to a better quality of life? As modern medicine advances, procedures are becoming less invasive, yet overall health is still on the decline. This begs us to find an alternative to these ways and getting back to the basic elements that make us up for answers.

While it is possible to attract positive energy to yourself, Reiki is most effective with a practiced healer, someone who is familiar with energy fields and has the ability to attract the most positive energy toward you. Remember that if your aura is weak, it will be hard to gather the strength to ask the universe for what you need. Don't be afraid to meet with a professional and give Reiki a try. Keep a positive, open mind going into the experience, and you won't regret it.

The benefit of Reiki is that it can help flush out the negative emotions and thoughts we have in our minds. Remember that positive energy is drawn to negative energy, and it will flow where it is needed most. The negativity may inhibit just how much energy we can accept, but it will work just the same. Having treatment frequently will help break down as much negativity as possible, eventually filling you with positivity.

Reiki is a very personal, unexplainable practice. If you have not had the pleasure of a Reiki session with a practiced Reiki master, it is highly recommended. We cannot truly explain in words the feeling of energy flowing through you, as this is a transcendental experience that will likely be different for each individual. You owe it to your inner spirit to try Reiki and find out the benefits for yourself.

Chapter 8: Practicing Reiki On Yourself

If you are new to Reiki and are intrigued by its benefits, meeting with a Reiki professional will be your best introduction to the practice. Find someone who is reputable and has lots of experience. It may seem like a strange new practice, but gaining the knowledge that this practitioner has is invaluable. Perhaps you will find that practicing with a professional is best for you, or maybe you would like to begin practicing on your own at home.

The energy that abounds in this universe can be drawn to any person, all we have to do is ask. For someone that is open and willing to ask will receive the benefits of this energy. Those who have this ability have the conscience to practice Reiki themselves. Even if this sounds like a transcendental version of you, it may surprise you to find that drawing energy to yourself is completely possible.

The great thing about working with a professional is that it allows you to relax and soak in the experience completely. The good news is, this can be mimicked at home. When you are first starting out on your own, you may not feel like you are getting much out of it. However, if you develop a routine of movements that become second nature to you, there will be no thought required to carry it out, giving the same effect.

Since you likely have more time available at home than traveling to see a practitioner, make Reiki something you practice at home every day as part of your routine. Just like exercise and eating right, practicing meditation and Reiki on a regular basis is part of preventative wellness. Doing these things proactively helps maintain the good health of our bodies now, instead of waiting to do something about it when ailments occur. The practice of Reiki is just that, practice. So practice every day.

Whether practicing at home or with a professional, it may get monotonous. After a while, it may feel like the same old thing, and the benefits may cease to exist for you. The idea behind any technique of energy healing is to keep your mind willing and open to accept wisdom from the universe. There is always something new to experience, so go into each session with an open mind, a curiosity and accepting nature.

Energy Healing

There are always different ways to practice as well. Perhaps you get bored with the current rotation in which you practice. It is okay to change it up and try something new. If you are guiding the energy in a different way, you are likely to get a new experience, which can keep the benefits rolling.

So, now that you have committed to trying Reiki every day, even for a short session, we may begin. While you will see an example Reiki session in the next chapter, we must first set the scene. As we discussed earlier, getting in the right mindset to accept energy from the universe is very important. If we are feeling stressed and negative, it will be hard to let that energy in.

It is recommended to practice a bit of meditation before getting started. Find yourself a quiet, comfortable space where it is comfortable in temperature, and moderately lit. Bright, fluorescent lights are not very calming, but if it is all you have, make it work. Another option is to forgo the lights and try candles for some dim lighting.

The five-minute meditation session in Chapter 14 is an ideal meditation session to try, as it only takes a few minutes, and quickly releases excess stress. Energy healing meditation does require a bit of focus on drawing energy, so this is a great start.

Once you have primed your body and mind for the energy, begin your Reiki practice. Your routine will be all your own, but in general, each touch point should be focused on for a set period of time to keep things flowing. If you are by yourself, it can be hard to focus on the time as well as the practice. Using recordings of gongs, and spiritual timer apps found online can help bring a bit of instrumental depth to your practice, while also keeping your session on track. Remember that if this is a daily occurrence, it will be hard to keep up if you regularly go outside your set time. Being late for work or other commitments will bring that stress flooding right back.

On that note, try to pick a time of day that will reasonably fit in your schedule. While we can do our best to stay on track, accepting energy and meditating with the universe is not a timed event. Yes, you can run on the treadmill for exactly a half hour to reap the benefits, but getting your mind to focus and accept energy cannot be done in a specified time frame. The universe is not keeping track of time, so it is unfair to ask it to give you what you need in short order. That is just selfish. If you find a time, say at the end of the day, where you are not infringing on any other commitments, you will feel freer to sit with the energy and accept it, rather than feeling rushed through.

Energy Healing

As discussed, finding your routine groove will be up to you. It may turn out that certain touch points do nothing for you, but others are remarkably energizing and healing. Remember that just as we must treat our entire chakra system, we should not focus all of our attention on certain points, as others may feel an energy imbalance in the process.

If you truly feel that certain practices are detrimental to your overall cause, try something else. There is no one routine that is best for everyone. The goal is to maintain balance in whatever routine you choose.

Chapter 9: Guided Reiki Self-Session

The order in which you choose to carry out your Reiki routine is up to you. Over time, you may find that making changes allows you to delve deeper into your spiritual being, and untap hidden healing potential. Use this guide as an example to get started. You are urged to do your own research and experiment with different techniques to find out what works best for you.

To get started, lie down in a comfortable position. On a bed, couch, or even the floor is just fine.

Close your eyes, breathing deeply in and out. Focus on your breath, clearing your mind of the thoughts of the day. With each exhale, feel the stress of the day flowing out of you.

Pause for 1 minute.

You should now feel relaxed. Now is the time to say a mental prayer to the universe, asking for the energy you need to fulfill your goals and heal your ailments. Ask it to send you only what you need. Feel this energy entering through the top of your head, flowing down to your healing hands. Feel the energy tingle in every finger.

Energy Healing

We are now ready to begin our Reiki session. Slowly bring both hands to your face, setting them gently on your closed eyes. Hold them there, feeling the energy flow through your hands, into the eyes.

Pause for 1 minute.

Slowly move both hands to the temples, resting them comfortably there. Focus as the energy flows into your brain through your temples.

Pause for 1 minute.

Move your hands now to your neck, where they will lay near your throat chakra. Feel the warmth of energy on your neck.

Pause for 1 minute.

Move your hands gently down to your chest, settling each hand over the lungs. As you breathe in and out, imagine that energy flowing in and out of each lung, surrounding the heart.

Pause for 1 minute.

Slide your hands slowly down to your abdomen, just above the navel. Your solar plexus chakra is where you will feel your confidence and self-worth. As energy flows to this area, imagine your inner worth increasing exponentially, as if ready to conquer the world.

Pause for 1 minute.

Slowly move both hands below the navel, to the sacral chakra. Feel the warmth enter your belly, enhancing your feelings of connection with those you love most. Think of them as you feel the energy flowing into this area.

Pause for 1 minute.

As you lay still, feel the pressure of the surface below you on your tailbone. As this root chakra is what is keeping you centered with the earth, feel that energy coursing in between both body and earth.

Pause for 1 minute.

Let your hands fall gently to your sides, resting comfortably. Focus on your breath, in and out.

Pause for 1 minute.

Take a moment to gather yourself and open your eyes. Slowly sit up, taking your time. It is time to re-enter the world refreshed, renewed and recharged.

Chapter 10: Finding happiness from within

While there are many types of energy healing, the benefits of all of them are a better sense of inner peace and connection with the universe. It is through this process that we can reconnect with our true self, and become able to accept help and guidance from our spirit. When we listen to the overwhelmingly loud signals our inner self gives us, we can make intuitive, educated decisions that lead us on a path to ultimate happiness.

Our inner self knows what will make us truly happy, and humans have gone on long enough ignoring its signs. If you are ready, it is high time you reconnect with your inner self, often called the inner child, who only operates on finding true bliss. Decisions are made based on happiness, not logic, and we definitely need more of that in the world.

The good news is, everything you need to be happy is already right inside of you. All of the misconceptions about tangible things like money and fancy things is only a fallacy. None of those things will make you happy, and so chasing after them is a waste of time. Perhaps you do have all of those things, but still feel a void in your life. While it is still important to be humble and appreciate the physical things that you have, it is time to explore what really makes you tick. Ask yourself this question; "When I wake up every morning, I do so in hopes of...". This open-ended question will help you discover what it is you are searching for, what gets you up and out of bed every morning.

In our new society, people are constantly trying to connect and be approved by other people. We have developed social media websites for the sole purpose of putting ourselves out there to be judged by others. We also value ourselves by how others see us, and by the opinions of people, we value the most. Many people are also dependent on a relationship with another as their source of happiness. A best friend or spouse can easily become a crutch, and happiness is dependent on whether or not that relationship is going well.

It is time to shift gears. We are each individually perfect just how we are. Our inner spirit is a glowing representation of our happiness, and it is time to let it out. We do not need to live for others, or for tangible things, we must live for ourselves. Once you begin thinking in these terms, the rest will fall into place. You will no longer be doing things for others that are of detriment to your inner self. For example, if a friend constantly takes advantage of your good graces, you will no longer feel the need to please them by being at their beck and call.

You will begin living your life as your spirit guides it. You will be able to find your true calling and find ways to make those dreams a reality. You will automatically be more relaxed, as you know your spirit is all-knowing, and you trust it will point you in the right direction. If this all sounds too good to be true, it is. The caveat is, you must be willing and able to ask the universe for this gift.

Remember that a positive, open mind will be able to accept energy and truly listen to its inner self. In order to make this a reality, we must focus our attention on it, ask for it, and seek it out. Nothing good ever just falls in your lap, and happiness is the same way. In your future meditation sessions, take a few minutes to set your mind on this stream of thought. Imagine that this positive energy is flowing to the areas of you that will be able to accept and make this image a reality.

Your happiness is entirely up to you. Do and think things every day that is happy, and you will have no other option but to be happy. Positive thoughts attract more positive thoughts. Be more mindful and conscious of the negative thoughts that creep into your day, and make an effort to turn them around and find the positive actively. Our brains are wired to continue thinking how you already think. It is easier to do the same thing over and over than to try something new. Exercise your brain and make it work on changing those negative thoughts around. Before long, you will find a happier you.

Chapter 11: Power of Positivity

The key to finding true happiness and living your best life is through positivity. Going through life with a negative attitude will only bring more negativity into your life. As we discussed in earlier chapters, it is hard for a person to accept positive energy from the universe when they have negative barriers up, keeping it out.

Negativity comes in many forms, and most are recognizable, entering your life on a daily basis. Sure, you may wake up in a good mood, but as soon as you punch that time clock, people are coming at you from all angles asking for things, draining your energy. You have two options. The first is to do what you have always done, talking to people in your standard exasperated tone, like everything they ask is a chore for you. What you will get in return is a negative attitude.

For example, let's say your co-worker asks you for the weekly sales report you compile every week. It has been a particularly stressful week, and it isn't quite ready at the time it usually is. This co-worker comes in looking for it, simply asking if it is ready, as the rest of their day depends on it. You respond with a long, drawn out explanation of what a horrible day you are having, and how it is really the last thing you need to worry about. Your poor co-worker stands there like a deer in the headlights, wondering what they did to have to put up with this explanation. In the end, this person really has nothing positive to say to you, and even tells your boss how unprofessionally you just acted. The day has nowhere to go but down.

The other option is to treat the situation positively. That is, the report is not done, your day has been hectic, and your co-worker is still asking for it. The situation has not changed, but the way you handle it can. Instead of the long, drawn-out explanation, you could simply say, "I'm a little behind today, I will work on the report next and forward it as soon as I have it. Sorry for the inconvenience." While you may not truly feel this way, the fact that you are positive about the situation will make your co-worker react in the same way (hopefully). The situation now has the possibility of having a positive outcome.

We often worry as well, and this is all just negativity. Going around wondering about the terrible 'what if' situations in life are unproductive and unnecessary. Worrying incessantly whether or not you will make it work on time, or if you will have a good day when you get there is a complete waste of time. None of us have any idea what is in store, so you might as well do yourself a favor and assume it will all be good. The universe will pick up on this positivity and send more good vibes your way.

Even when things do go wrong, which they will, training your mind to consider the silver linings in every situation is good practice. As we do not necessarily know the hidden plans of our inner self, there is no way to know whether a negative experience is really negative.

Consider for a moment your current job. Going in every day is a test of patience, and you leave every day feeling drained. Your performance is excellent, says your boss, but your heart just isn't in it. While you struggle to find meaning in work, you remain a good employee to keep the bills paid at home.

Deep down, you know this is not where you want to be, and your inner self knows it. Without realizing it, you are putting out a negative vibe about your situation and the universe is picking up on it. Suddenly, the company you work for makes a major shift, and you are laid off. While it would be easy to get upset, stressed and negative, it is just as easy to consider the situation a blessing, and an opportunity to find work that is more satisfying to your inner self.

Practice positivity every day to start seeing the good it will bring to your life. There truly is a silver lining in everything, even if we can't see it right away. Avoid the pitfalls of feeling sorry for yourself and instead plan your next move. Staying on the bright side of any problem will keep you from getting sucked down into a place full of anxiety and depression.

Chapter 12: Lowering Stress for Better Quality of Life

We have all heard about stress. A plethora of articles have been written about its detriment to health, and a quantity more have been written about how to reduce it. In reality, stress is a necessary part of life. Without it, nothing would ever get done. Stress is a physiological response meant to get your butt in gear

and away from bad circumstances. Going way back to early man, there were many more dangerous situations like animal predators and perils of weather living in primitive environments. When these situations arose, the body would naturally increase adrenaline, allowing the mind to be more attentive to the surroundings, and the body able to flee in case of disaster.

These days, there are much less dangerous things around in comparison. Our stress is usually work and family related, things we cannot simply run from. While we are relatively safe, stress is still useful to help get us to work, as the threat of not paying the bills can be just as devastating as a hurricane knocking down our tree hut.

The problem is, the stress indicator is naturally supposed to be met with action. In old times, stress would mean running from a predator, a physical response to the stimulus. Today, we are not physically doing much at all, and those stress hormones only sit in our bodies, wreaking havoc on our health and spiritual well-being, all at the same time.

One solution is exercise. If you are undoubtedly in a stressful situation that you cannot immediately leave, like being in debt and trying to figure out how to not be, regular exercise can help manage those unruly stress hormones. Daily walks or jogs, or yoga and Tai Chi can help move some of that pent up negative energy out, making room for more positivity.

Along with exercise comes a proper diet. Food is the fuel that keeps our bodies running smoothly, and therefore it is imperative to make sure we are fueling it well. Our fast-paced has led to the inception of fast food chains and junk food that give us very little nutritionally. Feeding our bodies with trans fats, added sugars, fats and preservatives that run rampant in these foods wreak havoc on our health. Nutritionally speaking, these substances are foreign. We are not meant to eat these things in excess, and the body has a hard time processing them.

Molecules from foods of unknown origin cause the immune system to become taxed as it tries to sort out "food" from the possible pathogen. Over time, stress hormones are released to help the immune system function properly, leading to weight gain and general inflammation in the body. It is this inflammation that is the root cause of most diseases, as research has recently discovered.

To take care of your body, fill it with hearty fruits and vegetables from natural sources. Organic is best as the produce will not be covered in harmful preservatives and pesticides. We also need to consume enough lean protein to ensure muscle maintenance, and the amino acid particles that make up protein are also necessary for a host of chemical reactions that keep the body going. Lean meats like chicken, beef, and fish are great, as well as plant-based sources like beans and nuts.

Our plates should mainly contain vegetables and lean proteins, but also a good source of carbohydrate from starches. Many of us overdo it on the starches, so this may be something you need to limit. As a guide, make about one-quarter of your plate starch. Pick them from good sources like potatoes and winter squash that are loaded with vitamins and minerals, instead of pasta and rice, which may have been stripped of nutrients.

Stress is all perceived by the mind, so we must not ignore meditation and mindfulness techniques as a solution. The mind is ultimately in charge of the body, and the release of stress hormones. If the mind says everything is okay, then the body will follow suit. Practicing daily positivity, meditation and Reiki will keep your mind calm, and help focus on solutions to your problem. Once there is a clear and concise plan, the brain really will be fine, and stress can be eliminated. In cases where a family member is ill, and the outcome is out of your control, daily meditation and positivity will keep stress at bay until something definitive happens.

This book has mainly been about ways to tap into your inner self for guidance, and it will be employed here as well. Listening for signals from your spiritual self will ultimately guide you in the right direction. However, we are also a creature that thrives on social contact. Employing guidance from trusted friends and family members goes a long way as well. It always helps to talk problems through with others, and who knows, maybe the universe is speaking through this person. Be open to the ideas given by others, as it could be the universe trying to get the message to you.

Chapter 13: Guided Imagery

Along with the idea of positive thinking is the concept of guided imagery. This practice is becoming more and more popular, not only because it is alternative and cost effective, but because it works. Sometimes the simplest ideas are the best.

Think about the last time you were reminiscent of a great experience. Perhaps you were gathered with friends and thought about that trip you all took last summer. How did it make you feel? You were likely excited, happy and feeling some emotional connection to that moment in time.

The mind is an amazing organ, in that its stored memories can bring you back to any given time, and cause you to feel the same way you did, even years before. We know this is true because we often regress to feelings from bad experiences. We often carry trauma from death, abuse, or even just a minor embarrassing moment that really stuck with you. Without realizing it, your mind is keeping these memories as lessons for next time. They are evidence that says, this situation didn't work out last time, so things are going to be different.

As the nature of this book is to make our lives better, let's use this idea to remember good times and boost your mood at this

moment using helpful information from the past. The practice of guided imagery is very simple. In clinical and therapeutic practice, it is the process of guiding a person to a better state of mind by focusing the brain on positive things. This can be done with a former pleasant memory, or with things that are pleasant in general, like picturing waves rolling onto the beach.

This technique is very common in therapy for patients with depression and anxiety. Creating a sense of calm and happiness through imagery helps the patient regulate their emotions and the hormones that cause them.

A guided imagery session is much like a meditation or Reiki session, in that the words spoken are meant to relax and soothe, so that the mind may focus in on something specific. The practitioner will take time to get the patient into an accepting state so that the therapy can be most effective.

Next, they will start setting the stage for the scene. The practitioner will begin to describe a picture. This could be the beach and waves, or something else that is known to soothe the patient. They will describe the color of the water, the foam that builds up as the waves crash, the sound of seagulls flying overhead. They will have them imagine the smell of the salt air and the feeling of the wind on their face. Anything and everything that allows the patient to be there at the beach, in a moment of calm, even if they happen to be in the midst of a panic attack.

The results are clear. This technique helps people calm themselves, and reach out from depression. Once a clear picture can be established it is possible for the patient to imagine these things on their own. In fact, any of us could easily do this for ourselves at home. Simply imagine something that makes you happy and calm, and imagine every aspect of its character.

Guided imagery can also be used for breaking habits or settling fears and anxieties. For example, if a person has a debilitating fear of small spaces, in that they cannot even ride an elevator without feeling claustrophobic, this technique may be able to help. The best way to conquer any fear is just to do whatever it is that makes you nervous. For this person, it could be riding the elevator.

However, if riding the elevator could cause this person to have a panic attack or other health-related problem, it would be a wise idea to start with guided imagery. A trained therapist could have this person imagine that elevator ride, instead of actually doing it. If done correctly, the patient will truly feel that they are in that elevator, and their emotions should be the same.

The problem is, this patient may feel the need to sabotage that elevator ride, imagining that it crashes to the bottom of the building in a blaze of fire. The job of the therapist would be to talk the patient through a positive outcome to their feared situation, rather than letting them worry and think the worst. Regular interventions with this type of therapy will eventually allow the patient to face their fears and move on with a normal life

No matter how you decide to use guided imagery, it can help you overcome fears, become happier and find a better quality of life. Even if you use it intermittently to escape from a tough work day, guided imagery is a positive, cost effective way to get your mind to a better state. Once there, you will be free to accept positive energy from the universe.

Chapter 14: 5-Minute Meditation

Welcome to this session of five-minute meditation. Because five minutes is such a short amount of time, this session will usually be reserved for calming and relaxation as a way to reduce stress. This routine is great if you are feeling anxious, and have just a few moments to gather your thoughts, like at work or before a big presentation. Let's begin.

Start by finding a comfortable sitting position in a quiet room.
Slowly close your eyes.
Breathe in, then slowly out.
Continue breathing deeply, in and out.
Pause
Focus your thought only on your breathing, in and out.
Pause
Let all of your stress and worry gather as you breathe in…
And as you exhale, feel all of that tension disappear.
Pause
Slowly bring your right hand to your abdomen, just above the navel.
Bring your left hand up next, cupping your right hand over your abdomen.
Pause

Sarah Rowland

Feel the slow rise and fall of your abdomen as you breathe in and out.
Focus on the feeling in your hands.
Feel the energy flowing through your fingertips to your abdomen.
Pause.

Open your eyes, still focusing only on your breath.
Put your arms down to your sides, slowly and deliberately.
Purposefully stretch your arms to the sky as straight as you can.
Reach those fingertips high, and accept new energy from the universe.
Feel it coursing through your fingertips.

Down your arms.
Into your abdomen, heart.
Down your legs, into the smallest toe.
Put your arms down to your side.
Take one more deep breath, in and out.
Now gather your new strength and energy.
You can now go forward with your day in strength and confidence.

Chapter 15: 30-Minute Meditation

Welcome to this session of thirty-minute meditation. Because we have some more time, this session will be dedicated to aligning your chakras and getting your mental state in order. Remember that your chakras need regular wellness checks to make sure they are working properly. While you may feel that one chakra, in particular, is in need of energy, do not forget that we must nurture our chakra system as a whole for proper function.

Start by finding a comfortable sitting position in a quiet room.
Slowly close your eyes.
Breathe in, then slowly out.
Continue breathing deeply, in and out.
Pause
Focus your thought only on your breathing, in and out.
Pause
Let all of your stress and worry gather as you breathe in...

And as you exhale, feel all of that tension disappear.

Pause

Let us begin healing our root chakra. Lean slightly backward, with your back straight, and the weight of your body putting slight pressure on your tailbone.

Imagine that your bottom is directly connected with the earth. As you breathe in and out, feel the energy flowing from the earth into your body, and your energy flowing toward the earth, interconnected. With this, let feelings of calm and centering overwhelm your body.

Breathe in and out.

Pause for 1 minute.

Lean back forward to your normal sitting position. Slowly bring both hands, cupped over one another, to your lower abdomen, just below your navel.

Feel the warmth of energy from your hands on your abdomen. Imagine energy from your fingertips making their way directly to your sacral chakra. With it allow feelings of love and energy course through you.

Breathe in, and out.

Slowly bring your right hand to your abdomen, just above the navel.

Bring your left hand up next, cupping your right hand over your abdomen.

Breathe in deep, and exhale fully.

Feel the positive energy of the universe flowing to your solar plexus. With this energy comes self-confidence and the overwhelming knowledge that you are wonderful, and perfect just as you are. You can accomplish anything in life.

Feel the slow rise and fall of your abdomen as you breathe in and out.

Focus on the feeling in your hands.

Feel the energy flowing through your fingertips to your abdomen.

Pause

Continue your deep breathing, in and out.

Slowly stretch your right arm across your chest, stretching it toward you with guidance from your left hand. Feel a good stretch across your back as you breathe in deeply, then exhale.

Pause for 30 seconds to stretch

Slowly stretch your left arm across your chest, stretching it toward you with guidance from your right hand. Feel a good stretch across your back as you breathe in deeply, then exhale.

Focus on your deep breath filling your lungs, and reinvigorating your heart chakra. Feel your heart beat slowly and methodically as you breathe in and out.

Pause for 1 minute.

Place your hands comfortably in your lap.

Bring your attention to your throat area. As you breathe deeply, in and out, imagine energy flowing up and down your windpipe, bringing energy and oxygen through this region. Know that your words are pure and truthful, as only good can come from this reinvigorated chakra. Continue breathing deeply, in and out.

Pause for 1 minute.

Feel that energy start to swirl up to your jaw, around your cheekbones, around your eyes and centering on your forehead, reaching your third eye. If comfortable, bring both hands up to your forehead and gently place them there. Feel the energy flowing into your third eye, filling you with wisdom and insight. With this energy, you have the ability to carry onward with your life, connected to your intuitions, guided by your inner self. Continue to breathe, in and out, slowly inhaling in fresh, bright new energy, and exhaling any stresses or anxiety. It is gone with your breath.

Pause for 1 minute.

Feel that bright energy raise up into the crown of your head, right at the very top. This spot is the highest point on your body and is closest to the sky. Accept the bountiful energy from the universe through this point. Imagine that a tiny string of light is coursing energy from the sun down into your body. It is here you feel most connected to the vastness of the universe, feel an unwavering connection with your spiritual being, and you are at one with the energy surrounding you.

Focus your attention on that energy. Feel it tingling at the top of your head. If you are willing to accept it, ask the universe for more energy. Feel it course down the back of your neck, down each vertebrae one at a time, overwhelming your chest and belly with warmth. Breathe deeply as it rushes all the way down to the bottoms of your feet, and through every toe.

Energy Healing

Continue breathing, in and out.

Pause for 1 minute.

Open your eyes, still focusing only on your breath.
Purposefully stretch your arms to the sky as straight as you can.
Reach those fingertips high, and accept new energy from the universe.
Feel it coursing through your fingertips.
Down your arms.
Into your abdomen, heart.
Down your legs, into the smallest toe.
Put your arms down to your side.
Take one more deep breath, in and out.
Now gather and focus your newfound strength and energy.
You can now go forward with your day in strength and confidence.

Conclusion

Thank you for making it through to the end of *Energy Healing: Heal Your Life with Chakra Healing, Reiki Healing, Guided Imagery, and Guided Meditation*. I hope it was informative and able to provide you with all of the tools you need to achieve your goals of spiritual enlightenment. This will be an ongoing process, and I am happy to have been a part of it.

The next step is to start trying some of these techniques in your own life and find out what works best for you. Lastly, if you enjoyed this book, I ask that you, please take the time to rate it on Amazon. Your honest review would be greatly appreciated. Thank you!

Crooked Holster

An Anthology of New Crime and Thriller
Writing

Crooked Holster

Editors: Jo Young, Sandra Kohls
Cover photography: Shanna L. Maxwell, SparkyInk photography
Typesetting: Sandra Kohls

ISBN-13: 978-1508819172
ISBN-10: 1508819173

CONTENTS

Crooked Holster

A big thanks to the tutors and students of the Department of Creative Writing at Glasgow University for their advice and support.

FOREWORD

'Crime can be found anywhere'. This is the watchword of Crooked Holster, a rather superbly named new anthology of crime writing produced by two MLitt students at Glasgow University. The mundanity of crime, the everyday-ness of it – these are good angles, I think. Too much crime writing is grandiose: serial killers with a dozen murders to their name before the story even starts; extreme, operatic sadists, whose tortures are described with a relish that says more about the writer than the character. Yet these kinds of books often fail to generate the charge of apprehension we feel when a stranger, walking towards us, makes eye contact, and keeps it up.

I have never (so far) been stabbed, shot or tortured, but I have experienced that adrenaline rush that comes from a white van driver nearly knocking me off my bike (and then swearing at me), or somebody walking too close behind me down a dark alleyway. I take note of these emotions, and I extrapolate from them when trying to describe the response of a fictional character to a much greater threat. I commend this exercise to all crime writers. Ask yourself: Was there more dread, tension, and sharp dialogue in my encounter with the shopkeeper who said I'd given him a ten when in fact I'd given him a twenty, than in the entire story I've just written about an axe murderer?

All these small-scale dramas I've been mentioning do not merely generate a sudden fight-or-flight shock, they also generate a furious moral balancing. Was I right to suggest that the shopkeeper was a 'F------ chancer' when it was possible he'd made a genuine mistake? And when he admitted his mistake, was his apology sufficiently grovelling?

Such everyday calculations should also be imported into crime fiction, which is a deeply moral medium. Its whole dynamic comes from the description of wrongs that need to be righted. This is what I once told a young policeman, who was giving out anti-crime fiction leaflets in a town hall where I was giving a reading. (The leaflets were headed something like, 'So you think crime's a game?') I would make the same point about morality to anyone tempted to look down on crime fiction, and crime fiction anthologies.

But the morality argument will not work with some doubters. These people simply think that crime fiction is inferior to literary fiction. I reply that a lot of literary fiction works on bluff. If people don't know what to make of something, they might decide that it's great. Crime fiction plays by known rules, and is readily judged by those rules. There is nowhere to hide. It is, in short, hard to write, and I welcome any new anthology that encourages its production, especially one that takes as its starting point the idea that, in crime fiction, small is…if not beautiful, then ugly in the right way.

Andrew Martin
London, February 2015

Andrew Martin is a journalist and novelist. His critically praised 'Jim Stringer' series began with *The Necropolis Railway* in 2002. The following titles in the series, *Murder at Deviation Junction* and *Death on a Branch Line*, were shortlisted for the CWA Ellis Peters Historical Crime Award and, in 2008, Andrew Martin was shortlisted for the CWA Dagger in the Library Award. *The Somme Stations* won the 2011 CWA Ellis Peters Historical Crime Award.

Not a Wink Since Labor Day

Sarah Palmer

Tonight I need my beauty sleep like a Martini needs vermouth. So the moron trying to knock a hole through my apartment door's getting me kinda vexed. Nate's still out cold under my best goose-down comforter. Nathan Bernard, barman extraordinary at the Trip Trap Club on Mulberry - an occasional slip who's turning into a nasty little habit. Soon he'll be sending me roses and planning weekends upstate. Time for me to find a new place to drink. Love's for showgirls, and princesses, and women who can cook without reaching for a Betty Crocker mix. Not broads like me.

The moron's still knocking, and now it's getting loud. According to the pale face of my wristwatch it's 3.09am - whoever's come visiting isn't on a social call. I grab my pearl-handled Smith & Wesson .38, my mother's old gun, and stash it in the pocket of my robe. You can't be too careful in this city. I've taken enough crime scene photos, enough mug shots of crooks and thieves and murderers in my time to earn myself a suitcase full of enemies.

I shoulda known it. Detective Joseph Johnson of NYPD's Homicide Division is hanging on my door frame, flanked by his loyal coterie of patrolmen – Irish Mike, Russian Frank, and the small guy from the Bronx who's mother must have once gotten friendly with a mule.

It doesn't matter if it's 3.09 am or pm, Johnson's always dressed the same – rumpled brown suit, dirty black shoes, and a hang-dog face sucking on the smouldering remains of a Lucky Strike.

'Hey, Eloise,' he says, not even bothering to take the cigarette from his lips. 'Sorry 'bout the hour but we gotta stiff over in

Briarwood. You betta get dressed.'

Johnson and I have a past. A long passed past, but one he has trouble forgetting. He stares through me into the bedroom and shakes his head,

'Nathan Bernard, huh?' he says. 'Can't mix your own cocktails these days?'

He never can resist an opportunity. But then again, neither can I.

'How's your wife, Joe?'

Johnson shrugs his shoulders and turns to the patrolmen,

'Come on, guys, let's give the lady some privacy.' He heads for the stairwell. 'See you in the car, ma'am,' he says. 'Don't keep us waiting, now.'

The house is on a neat-looking plot on a regular street in a pleasant enough neighborhood. So suburban it could be baking a cake. Only the row of black and white Plymouths lined up alongside the lawn show it's not ordinary no more. A small group of neighbors has gathered at the end of the pathway, mainly middle-aged women in their slippers and housecoats. Some smoking, some looping loose strands of hair up into their pin curlers. Like a line of derelicts at a pajama party.

I take a few pictures for the record. You never know who could be out there pretending to be an innocent bystander, when just hours before they've been playing fast and loose with the victim's life.

The crowd startles as the flash bulb explodes. When the negatives are printed, you can bet they'll all look guilty as hell.

`Hey, ma'am, our business's inside,' Edwards says. `Quit trying out for your New Yorker profile, wilya?'

I duck by the flowerbeds and go inside the house. Patrolwoman O'Flaherty's making coffee for a dumpy woman who's sobbing at the kitchen table. Whenever there's a big case, O'Flaherty is there, making coffee, taking care. Someone once told me she has

5

kids. Who knows how she found the time to make them.

Johnson nudges me on his way to the stairs.

'Our suspect, I guess' he says, nodding towards the weeping woman.

O'Flaherty pours two spoonfuls of sugar in her cup.

In the bedroom, a naked white man lays on his back across the unmade bed. A thick blond pelt covers his body, a body that looks like it enjoyed more than one beer and chilli dog in its time.

No need to ask about the murder weapon - a chintzy pillow's covering his face. I start to take pictures as Johnson pushes the pillow aside onto the mattress, getting close up to photograph the vic's livid complexion, his ginger stubble, the floral comforter. The absence of blood at the scene makes a kinda pleasant change.

'Crime a passion,' Johnson's saying. 'Seen it a hundred times. The guy seems happily married, but he talks in his sleep. Says the name of another woman again and again. First time, she's ignored it, put it down to a bad dream. But tonight he's been out late, comes back stinking of beer. And when he wakes the wife up, muttering that name again…' He shrugs. 'Open and shut case.'

I'm still taking pictures. It's a familiar room scene with a closet, chest of drawers, and a pile of pantyhose and singlets lying on a chair like a showgirl's discarded gloves. The nightstands are the same in every household across New York. Sitting on the victim's are a pack of Chesterfields and last week's National Enquirer. Face cream, a diced makeup sponge and a small brown pillbox are arranged on what must be our suspect's. I get in close and photograph the label.

'Sleeping pills,' I say. 'Hey, Joe, I'm not disagreeing with you about the wife, but I don't think you're right on the motive.'

'No?'

His face says he is.

'No. It all makes sense. Let's go speak with the widow.'

She's still sobbing at the kitchen table, not noticing the

—

6

uniforms standing around, drinking cups of coffee and flirting with O'Flaherty.

I pass her a Kleenex. 'It was the snoring, wasn't it,' I ask.

She looks up at me with red-rimmed eyes. Some of her tear tracks have dried to salt, like a thirsty riverbed in a Godforsaken land. Woulda made a fine picture.

'Whaddya mean, snoring?' she says.

'It's laid out on your nightstand. The sleeping pills. That makeup sponge is chopped up small enough for the fairies. Or for a grown woman to put into her ears at night. He was a man who could sleep through an earthquake – but not you. Am I right?'

Pulling her housecoat closer, she begins to rock.

'You shoulda heard him. When we first married, it wasn't so bad. The snoring was kinda quiet, and it only happened when he slept on his back. All I had to do was slip my hand underneath him, roll him over...'

She's demonstrating the hand movement. Johnson lights another cigarette.

'But over the years he started to drink more, he got fat...' she sighs. 'In the last six months, it got so bad. Not just snoring on his back, but his left side, his right side, his front... It was like an airplane coming into land.'

The crying starts again,

'Not even the Nembutal could drown it out. I haven't had a good night's sleep since Labor Day.'

Johnson's right beside her,

'Why didn't you go sleep in the spare room,' he says. 'Save you killing the man?'

'The spare room? It's a shrine to his mother. Not even a priest'd try to spend the night in there.'

She'll sleep well in the cells tonight alright. 'I'm sorry for your loss,' I say.

Edwards snorts. 'Good call, Eloise. Take her downtown,' he says to Russian Frank. 'And O'Flaherty, get me another coffee willya?'

O'Flaherty winks at me as she turns to the faucet. There are no female sergeants in the NYPD. I hope I'm looking at the first.

I hadn't refused Johnson's offer of a ride back into the City, because a hangover was starting to brew like something outa Macbeth. But I shoulda taken on the weird sisters – anything would be better than Johnson reaching out for my thigh.

'You're still a beautiful woman,' he says, the air around his head filling with the smoke of his twentieth Lucky Strike.

I push his hand away.

'What's a creep like Nathan Bernard got that I haven't?'

Like he has to ask.

The sky's starting to lighten as I get back to my building. Climbing the stairway I think about making coffee, but it's dark inside the apartment and beauty sleep starts singing me a lullaby.

Nathan stirs as I slip under the comforter, but doesn't wake. I lay against his warm body, taking in the sounds of the city at dawn. A fire truck, the crash of pans at the bakery across the street, two cats getting friendly in the trash.

But inside the apartment, my bed, it's as quiet as a synagogue at Christmas. Only the rise and fall of Nathan's chest against my shoulder blades tell me he's still breathing.

Seems even broads like me have to settle down sometime. After all, there aren't many men in this city who can mix a Gimlet that dances in your throat like stockings in the breeze, and one of them's sleeping silently beside me.

As long as he takes a pledge to stay away from the suburbs, Nathan Bernard might get to send me roses after all.

Booties

B. D. Lamont

'Well that was easy.'

Tony glared up at Georgie, wishing he had the energy to slap him. 'You, yeh *stupit* -' Tony had to stop before he passed out. He was bent over at the mouth of the lane they'd just sprinted down. Moonlight didn't stand a chance between the neon sign of the tattoo parlour and the kebab shop across the street. The green and pink lights picked out the slick cobblestones beneath Tony's trainers. His hands gripped his shaking knees. He was trying to will the gutter into focus. He swallowed the city air and his lungs spat it out.

Georgie pulled the stolen shopping trolley towards him. It veered to the side and bumped against the wall of the lane, jostling its contents: cardboard boxes and hunks of computing equipment.

'Georgie . . . See when this is done. You,' Tony pointed a finger at him, 'you better no even *think* of contactin' me again. I'll fuckin' throttle you, so I will. *Christ.*' Tony screwed his eyes shut trying to slow down his breathing. He couldn't collapse now. Not in front of this eejit.

'Come on, how was I supposed to know the scaffolding had been taken down, like? That ward has been closed off for weeks. I checked.'

'When?'

'Two weeks ago.'

'Two -?! Fuckin' hell, yeh were supposed tae scope out that bit las' night! Told you tae gee it a once over, I mean are yer ears fuckin' painted oan?' Tony's knees gave up and he eased himself down onto the damp footpath lining one side of the lane.

Yeah, but if you hadn'tve been in such a rush, like, you'dve seen the Do Not Enter sign. You're pretty spritely for an old man y'know. I tried to catch up and tell you about the sign, and to stop like, but...'

'You said you'd just seen the polis outside. 'Course am gonnae be fuckin' rushin'! Bit preoccupied to be reading' signs. Ah nearly went through that hospital windae thinkin' there wis a scaffoldin' to catch me! Could've fell and broke my neck. Had to turn aroon, din't we? Go back all that way to the lab. Then yeh go and knock that bloody crash unit doon the stair just as we manage to find our way oot that fuckin' rabbit's warren.' Tony took a moment to glare at Georgie who was scuffing his brand new Nike Airs into the dirt between the cobbles.

'Was an okay plan, I thought.'

'Am thinkin' the fact that our planned escape route no existing anymare might be a wee hiccup in your fuckin' genius plan. Nearly ran right out into fuck all. Runnin' like a fanny because you cry polis! Jesus.'

'Well I thought it *was* the police, alright?'

Tony glowered at him.

'Well, I thought it went rather smoothly. A part from those little . . . hiccups.' He looked down at Tony and attempted one of his winning smiles. 'We made it didn't we? And we got what we came for! Look,' he pointed to the trolley, 'we have just acquired a *six* figure cash bonus for an hour's work!' Georgie was grinning down at him. Tony didn't care if he passed out; he was gonnae plant his fist right into tha' smug face, the inconsiderate wee cu-

A gurgling sound came from the trolley.

'Whit.' Tony coughed, hocked what felt like a piece of brain matter onto the cobbles, and groaned. 'Whit wis tha'?' Tony managed to stand up. 'Thought yeh said the machines were aff?'

'They are.' Georgie glanced at the trolley and shrugged. 'Well they *were* off. Probably knocked one of them too hard while we were running down the alley.'

Techno music blared into the lane.

Georgie patted down his sports jacket before pulling out his mobile phone and answering it. 'Hello? Yeah, hi. . . Uh huh.' Georgie frowned and turned away.

Tony could feel his blood simmer. He couldn't believe it; that eejit had his phone on maximum fuckin' volume the *the whole fuckin' time?!* Tha' wis it. Never again. God as his witness, he wasnae doin' this again, this wis the last job. Mags warned him he'd have a heart attack before he wis fifty. She said tha' who else wis she gonna moan at? Nae kids, nae grandkids. Still, he had to prove her wrang. Oh aye, well done big man. Score this job and die of a blown artery before he even got the cash in his bank account. Aye very clever.

Georgie hung up the phone. 'That was our pick up guy.'

'Right. Whit's he wantin'?'

'Well he's, er, ran into a spot of bother.'

'Christ, he's no coming is he?'

'Um, no.'

'Right. Great.' Tony walked up to the trolley and turned to Georgie. 'We've nae van, we've both left our motors at hame, we cannae take this oan the bus, can we?' Tony sighed. 'Whit now?'

A wail rose up from the trolley. Tony stumbled backwards. Georgie dropped his phone and it fell apart on the cobbles.

'Ah for fff-'

The wailing grew louder. Tony lifted the flap of one of the boxes. Amongst the thick black cables and bubble wrap was a baby.

Tony stared at its smooth pale chest undulating with the effort of crying. 'Nae chance.'

A small rag or blanket had been laid underneath it. Just the corners of it could be seen beneath its shoulders. The baby opened its mouth over and over again, gulping down air between wails, revealing a neat row of tiny pearly-white teeth. *Teeth?* Tony thought, but was hauled back to the imminent danger of being discovered by Georgie yanking him by the shoulders.

'Tony! Do something!'

Tony shoved a near-hysterical Georgie off him. 'Like whit?'

'I don't know! Make it stop!'

'How?'

'Someone's going to hear us, Tony please!'

'*How* Georgie?'

'I DON'T CARE! JUST SHUT IT UP!'

He stared at Georgie, his eyes wide. The neon lights out in the street flickered. A car screeched and rocketed past the lane.

Tony placed his hands into the box and picked up the baby, blanket and all. Georgie made to move towards him. 'Tony, listen, like, I didn't mean to - just don't hurt it.'

Tony shot him a look and Georgie stepped back. Tony's rough hands easily covered the baby's back as he held the writhing body up for a moment. He brought its struggling form to his chest.

'Shhh, shhhh, 'mon now, it's okay.' He cradled the baby and, very slowly, rocked on the balls of his feet. Georgie looked like he was going to say something but Tony just shook his head. He closed his eyes, letting the anger evaporate into the city air. He hummed and muttered softly under his breath, watching as tiny pink fingers grasped at nothing. It sniffled, no longer wailing just gurgling. It looked up at Tony with big dark eyes.

Georgie cleared his throat.

'Whit? You never seen a bairn before Georgie?' Tony smiled for the first time that night. He shifted his fingers to get a better grip and noticed the blanket wasn't a blanket at all. 'Whit's this, then?' Tony very gently turned the baby round.

'Are those -?' Georgie stepped up and peered at the baby's back. 'Oh my God.'

'Naw.'

'They're. Those are . . . '

'Ah, Fuck.'

The feathers were soft and small. They felt silky beneath Tony's hands. Long sinewy folds merged into the tufts that lined its shoulders and curved along either side of its spine just the curve of it shoulder blades. One or two tiny feathers slipped loose where

---

12

Tony's callouses caught them and they floated down like snow.

'Georgie,' Tony hissed. 'Whit yeh doin?'

'What does it look like?' Georgie's words were somewhat muffled as he rummaged through the contents of the trolley.

'Looks like yeh've lost yer bloody marbles. You hoping for another bird-bairn? Make a matching set and sell the lot oan Egay?'

'God, it's E*bay* and no.' he yanked on something amongst the boxes. 'Looking for – ah!' Georgie retrieved a bulging file from the depths of the trolley. He beckoned Tony over, balanced the file on the cardboard boxes and opened one of the files. 'I want to know what we're dealing with, like. I mean it's a bit of a coincidence that we get asked to steal all this computing crap and there's a . . . a baby. Kind of. Smuggled among all the other stuff. I think that little guy is part of the cargo.'

A chill wind blew through the lane. Papers fluttered from the file and Georgie scrambled to catch them. Tony's phone vibrated in his back pocket. 'Shit.' Tony fumbled with one hand to extract his phone and not drop the baby who was now clutching at the thin fabric of his shirt. Small strong fingers found a nipple. "Ah! Yeh wee bastart." He shoogled the baby higher up against his chest and answered his phone, crushing it between his neck and shoulder. 'Hullo? Oh. Hi darlin'...'

Georgie had fit most of the documents back into the file. He stooped down to pick up the last one. 'Tony,' he said, the paper shaking in his hand.

'Naw, A'm fine, just a wee bit too much excitement sweetheart, think this'll be my last.' He looked up to glare at Georgie but the look on Georgie's face brought him up short. 'Aye . . . naw, listen A'm nearly done here, I'll, eh, I'll gee yeh a wee ring oan my way hame darlin'. Aye, love you too. Right, bye.' He grabbed the phone with his free hand and shoved it in his back pocket. 'Whit is that Georgie?'

Georgie's face had gone the same colour as the white leaf fluttering in his hands. His lips were pressed in a thin line as he held it out for Tony to see.

Pictures. Two of them at the top and a small one at the bottom of the page with lines of typed text in the middle. Some words were highlighted, some crossed out in pen. Notes had been made down the side. The baby was featured in all three. In the top left it was lying on its back, with a tiny hospital tag on its fat wrist. It looked normal, Tony thought. And it's a boy. He wondered how he never noticed before. Oh aye, Tony thought, the wings.

In the top right picture, the baby had been lain on its stomach, its arms flung out either side as if reaching for something. Someone had taken hold of its wings, stretching them out. They only reached his elbows and trailed down to his tailbone. The third picture at the bottom was of a crumpled little creature curled up and apparently screaming, if the wide open mouth and the lines creasing its face were any indication. Its arms were pierced in several places by needles with tubes attached and extending out past what the picture showed. Minute electrodes were dotted in blue and green all over its chest and back, its wings were pinned together, squashed against its spine, and feathers were strewn around it on the hospital bed.

Tony looked down at the creature. Clear wet spittle bubbles burst from its pudgy mouth.

'What are we going to do Tony?'

Before Tony could say anything, his phone vibrated in his back pocket again.

'Christ, cannae get a minute's peace. Told her I'd gee her a ring . . . Aye, look sweetheart something's happened, I'll – oh. Eh, hullo sir."

Georgie winced and grabbed his hair.

'Aye, the job's done, nae problem.'

Georgie looked close to tears, shaking his head and waving his arms like a crazed flight controller. Tony motioned for him to be quiet. 'Mm, aye, all went well . . . Suspicious?' He glanced at Georgie, who now looked as if he was on the verge of slamming his head against the wall. 'Nah, nothin' like that. Look we've got yer gear, when do you want it droapped aff?' The baby was twisting in his grip. Tony jerked his head and Georgie stopped pacing and came over. Tony held out the baby.

'No way!' Georgie mouthed but Tony thrust the baby at him anyway. Georgie took it at arm's length. It kicked and flailed but remained quiet.

Tony covered the mouthpiece of the phone. 'Georgie fuckin' hold it yeh tadger!'

Georgie made a face but held it close to his shoulder and bobbed it up and down.

'Aye, yeah of course. Nae worries . . . another job?' Tony's knuckles paled holding his phone. '*How* much? . . . Och I appreciate the offer anawl but my wife's kicking up shit as it is – ha, yeah . . . naw cheers anyhoo. Aye. A'm positive.'

Tony hung up. He took the baby off Georgie.

'Well?' Georgie said.

'Well, yer man says we'll get the cash next week.'

'But what about – y'know, *this?*'

Tony sighed. He felt the baby's warmth through his shirt. 'Christ. I dunno… Mags always wanted a bairn.'

The Job

Wendy H. Jones

Sunday lunch is sacrosanct in my family. Always has been. Everyone gathered together, no exceptions, no excuses. Church first and then rush back to sit and eat the mouth-watering fare my wife puts down in front of us. Tantalising smells titillate the taste buds and make them zing. Anticipation is high as we wait for grace to finish so we can take the first ambrosial bite. What's that you say? My family. Of course, let me introduce them. My wife, the beautiful Claire, mother extraordinaire and Cordon Bleu Chef. My oldest, James aged twelve, sensitive and artistic, with talents he received as a gift from his mother's genes. Pianist's hands. Meet Arabella, aged ten, serious and studious, nose in a book as she shoves tortoiseshell glasses up her very feminine nose. Louisa is five, all bright red curls and a smile the size of Scotland. The twins, nine months old, they babble all day long. Laughing at jokes only they understand. Wait, don't go just yet. There's someone you've still to meet. Sammy. Eight years old, bright as a button and inquisitive about everything. He is the sort of boy who would strip your computer just because it was there. My study is double locked against Sammy. Too inquisitive by far so it's better to make sure the place is safe from prying hands.

    'Daddy. Why were you out before church?' Yep, that's Sammy, interrupting my reverie.

    'Daddy had to go to work.'

    'But it's Sunday. You shouldn't work on a Sunday. The bible says that's bad.'

    'That's right Sammy. It does. But some people need to work on a Sunday.'

    'What's your work Daddy?'

'I'm a contractor.'

'What's a contractor?'

'Someone who helps people do things that they can't do themselves.'

'So if you help me build my train set. You're a contractor?'

'In a way. Yes.'

'How do you make money to buy my train set then? I don't give you any money.'

That's Sammy. Always asking questions. Never satisfied with the answers.

How do I make money? My mind drifts away from the lunchtime chatter. It replays my last job in vivid, dazzling, Technicolor. It had been planned for many weeks. Each step worked out and practiced until fluid. It had come to fruition that morning leaving me with a glorious sense of self-satisfaction over a job well done.

Step one of the planning had been to survey the landscape. I needed to know every inch of the terrain. Each crack in the pavement was studied and memorised. There wasn't a shop or a house that hadn't been committed to memory. If there was a bin, a post box or a phone box I knew about it. I could tell you the route and time of every bus within a radius of a few miles. I needed to know this area better than I knew my own family. Better than I knew myself. My success depended on it. My job is exhilarating. More exhilarating than your average Joe would ever know. But it is also endless days and nights of boring, tedious scutt work. Preparation is crucial in my line of work. Lack of knowledge can mean the difference between success and failure. It can mean the difference between being paid and receiving nothing. I am a master craftsman who leaves nothing to chance. Like an artist who prepares his canvas, I prepare my landscape.

This morning it was time to complete the job. Up and out

before the birds start singing. Dressed in clothes, which, though warm, are light and allow free movement. My limbs have to be responsive and ready. The tools of my trade are cradled lovingly inside a padded bag. Expensive tools made of the finest quality materials, strong and yet light. The best that money can buy. I am acknowledged as being unsurpassed at my trade. This reputation is not gained by using substandard materials. Arriving at my destination I set up. Methodically I screwed together, and test, each of the component parts. Ready, I watched and waited. patient. No use spoiling things at that point. At just the right moment a slight movement of my finger and my job is done. I packed up and left satisfied that there is one less paedophile in this world. Satisfied also that there will be a hefty sum landing in my offshore bank account.

'Daddy. You're not listening. How do you make money?'
Sammy's voice drags me back to the room and my rare roast beef.
'I help people clear up rubbish Sammy.'

Knox and the Reformers

David McVey

A tinkle of breaking glass in the gloom, a brittleness echoing through the empty house, dark as a November midnight can make it. A door opens, unleashing more echoes; light footfalls are muffled by the carpet tiles. There's a fumbling of wires and the snap of plugs being disconnected, and a slim oblong object is seized by the dark, liquid form of the intruder. The door is left open when he leaves. The house is silent again, though a car engine pulses into life, more easily heard through the open door, were there anyone there to hear it.

✪

'It should be a splendid lecture,' Knox announced as we sped, late, into the auditorium.

I offered a pained smile. It was one of the busiest times of the University year; marking, exam boards and progression panels were under way and there were papers to polish for forthcoming conferences. Knox had needed to cajole me into joining him at this inconveniently-scheduled town and gown lecture, uninvitingly entitled *Scotland's Reformation; 450 Years On*.

Suddenly, Knox stopped and turned to me, as if he had heard my thoughts; 'Dr Garvald Punks is a celebrated authority on Scotland's civil and ecclesiastical history, Malky. I should have expected that the opportunity to hear such an eminent figure would appeal to someone of even your shallow and vacillating views.' And then he sidled along a row and found seats, with me trailing behind like a chastened schoolboy. It often happened when I was with Knox.

Annoyingly, Knox was right; Dr Punks knew his stuff and communicated with clarity and gusto, making allowances for an audience many of whom were not religious history zealots. I had feared he might be a stern Presbyterian of Knox's stamp, but he was cool and objective towards his subject, though rather more positive about the cultural impact of the Scottish Reformation than I'd expected.

'And so we leave the Reformation in Scotland,' he concluded, '450 years on. Is it over, is it relevant, is it contentious? To fully answer those questions, I'd need to recite my entire book, *Scotland's Reformation and its Impact*. Copies are, of course, available for purchase!'

The chairman thanked the speaker and invited questions from the audience. There were a few enquiries of a technical, recondite kind, far above the head of a simple lecturer in Forensic Science. And then Knox stood up.

'Dr Punks, I gather that Professor Garth Collymoon is also producing a history of the Scottish Reformation. Have you been in contact with him?'

A chill seemed to pass over Garvald Punks; his smile faded, he stiffened his posture and replied in a serious tone, 'I am aware that Dr Collymoon has expressed such an intention, but no, we have not been in touch.' The frostiness seemed to spread to the audience and there was a palpable lack of buzz for a spell, before the next questioner stood up and asked something less threatening.

Afterwards, I drove Knox to the station. 'What did you think of that?' he asked, his long, spindly arms wrapped around his bony knees, which were lifted high as usual so that he could fit into my wee Fiat.

'Intriguing,' I answered, cagily, 'And I'll ask you the same question when I drag you to an organic chemistry conference.'

'Ah,' he said, 'I shall look forward to it.' My heart sank; it was true, Knox, who had a life sciences background before he

—

entered the ministry, probably *was* likely to be fascinated by organic chemistry. 'Did you notice his response to *my* question, though?' he went on.

·'I did, actually. Really got to him, you old rascal, didn't you? Is there some kind of scholarly punch-up going on between him and the Collymoon fella?'

'Punch-up?' said Knox, shaking his head, 'What a Runyonesque view you take of the simple academic life, Malky. But, yes, they *are* rivals with a long history. However, there will be no competing histories of the Scottish Reformation any time soon. Garth Collymoon's laptop, containing all his work, was stolen some months ago.'

I stopped the car at the kerb outside a Cathcart Circle station, turned to Knox and said, 'You didn't invite me tonight because of Punks' dazzling speaking; you're on a *case!*'

Knox grinned - always an unearthly sight - and climbed out of the car. Before he walked away, he motioned for me to wind down the window and said, 'we're going to speak to someone else tomorrow - I'll meet you outside your office at 5pm.'

I had been intending to stay late in my office next day to work on a conference presentation after a day of meetings, panels and marking, but Knox swept off and disappeared down the station steps before I could protest against this peremptory summons.

I'm Professor Malcolm Kennedy, by the way, of the University of South Glasgow. Long ago, Knox was a postgrad researcher in the university's Zoology Department and that's when I got to know him. Tall, bald-skulled, thin and bony, his austere appearance concealed a dry wit and a slyness some might suggest was at odds with his status as an ordained minister.

When he appeared at my office next day, he wore as usual a black suit, a shirt with a clerical collar and a long, severe, black woollen overcoat. This was June, remember, but Knox never seemed to feel the heat, or, indeed, the cold.

'So what gripping experience related to dead religious people are we about to enjoy now?'

'Malky,' said Knox, 'I do believe sarcasm may be your besetting sin.'

We drove to one of Glasgow's meaner post-war housing estates, far out to the north-east, a frustrating stop-start journey of traffic lights and busy streets and congested roundabouts. Knox didn't drive and often imposed on me when he needed to get somewhere that required too complex a linking of bus routes. The very thought of taxi fares seemed to outrage his Presbyterian sense of thrift.

To my surprise, Knox directed me towards a squat Roman Catholic church; we parked outside and Knox led me to a small house in the grounds. He pressed a doorbell and soon a small, shaggy-haired man in his thirties, wearing a clerical collar, answered. 'Well, would you believe it?' he said in a strong Irish accent, 'It's Knox the emotionally-repressed apostate! Have my superiors not burned you at the stake yet?'

'Enough of the surprise, Gilbert,' said Knox, 'You knew I was coming. Let's get in and get the kettle on.'

Shortly after, over a hefty potful of tea, I was introduced to Father Gilbert Ryan. 'Gilbert and I often meet up,' said Knox, 'for a social chat in which I endeavour to correct Gilbert's views on the papacy, transubstantiation, the veneration of saints and that kind of thing.'

'You clerics certainly know how to party,' I observed.

'We first met on a Radio Scotland programme,' said Ryan, 'debating the legacy of Knox's sixteenth century namesake. As on every occasion when we foregather, not only was I in the right, but I won the argument.'

They settled down after a while and Knox explained about Collymoon, his Reformation work, and the theft of the laptop.

'Has he contacted the police?' asked Ryan.

'No,' said Knox, 'he preferred that I should investigate on his behalf without involving the authorities. I consider this to be an instructive point.'

'Must have been a lot of work involved,' mused Ryan, 'He hasn't published a lot of papers lately. All his efforts going into the book, I suppose.'

'What's the history between Punks and Collymoon?' I asked.

'Collymoon is generally quite critical of the Reformation,' said Ryan, 'and of course I like that in a person. Punks is more measured, perhaps even positive. But their feud has nothing to do with history or theology. They were colleagues at St Andrews and fell out over the usual things; claims about stealing ideas, intellectual property and all that. Their differences in viewpoint are a symptom of their feud, not a cause.'

Ryan lit a cigarette and smiled with relish as Knox wrinkled his nose and drew his seat back some distance, towards an open window. 'Tell you what, though,' said Ryan, 'Last time I heard of Collymoon, a fellow-priest saw him coming out of his local college one Saturday lunchtime. He'd been at a pottery class. What do you make of that?'

We all sat quietly for a while, the Presbytery clock ticking out time. From the midst of the gloom and silence I asked, 'We're not actually accusing Garvald Punks of nicking the laptop, are we?'

Knox thought for a moment before speaking; 'No, I do not think we can do that. He would gain nothing; his book will not sell more for being the only new work on the topic.'

I said, 'And if Punks or anyone else stole it, why not call in the police?'

'It's incompetent of Collymoon not to have had a backup,' said Ryan.

More silence, then I asked, 'What does Collymoon actually want you to do, Knox?'

'There I think you strike upon the very heart of the matter, Malky. What indeed? Why me, and not the police? Why someone in the ministry and not the guardians of law and order?'

Ryan and myself must have looked rather battered by this

onslaught of rhetorical questioning, so Knox stood up smartly and added, 'I must go and speak again to Collymoon, and this time you will come with me, Malky.'

A few days later, Knox and I stood in a stark room in a bland suburban villa, fitted out with plain office furniture standing on cheap carpet tiles. A new laptop sat, switched off, on a desk of fake walnut, linked by the usual wiry spaghetti to a mouse, a printer and a broadband connection. Perched on the furniture were several clumsily-executed, crudely-fired pieces of pottery.

'Professor Collymoon, I'd like you, for Malcolm's benefit, to describe again the theft of your laptop last winter.'

The man who had admitted us to the house had cut a comical figure; fleshy, round, with a matching circular, jowly head. He was bald and affected tiny spectacles with black-rimmed round frames of the kind you often see in pre-war photographs. He showed us into this study, and it was only when he opened his mouth that the impression of an unemployable simpleton was exploded. 'Welcome, gentlemen' he'd said, 'to my sanctum and scriptorium.'

Now, he furrowed his brow irritably at having to re-tell his story. He and his wife had been visiting friends and they had returned to find the glass door leading into the study to be open, a pane smashed in order to access the lock, and the laptop vanished. As the most likely explanation, he suggested a scenario like that with which I began this account.

'Well, you have a new laptop, eh? PC World?' said Knox, heartily.

'No. A local firm.'

'Shame you didn't keep backups,' I suggested.

'Professor Kennedy, like you, I use computers. But I do not love them. I do not understand all the ins and outs of their functioning and non-functioning.'

'Well, you understand about the importance of backing up your work, now, at least,' said Knox, with his horrible smile. The doughy planes of Collymoon's face shifted to display something which was, I think, also intended as a smile. 'Have you begun the new version of the book?' Knox persisted.

'There were 150,000 words on that laptop,' complained Collymoon, spreading his arms wide in a gesture of helplessness, 'and all my references and sources. How could I possibly begin again?'

Knox thought for a moment and continued, 'There will have been quite a few papers and other works in progress on the equipment as well?'

'I don't understand.' said Collymoon.

Knox smiled again. 'I suppose not. In recent times you have concentrated solely on your book. Perhaps to the detriment of your ability to publish in the academic journals?'

Collymoon scowled, while I sat on a hard plastic chair in the corner, a mere onlooker as Knox pressed his points.

'After all, to the end of 2009 you published over 250 articles in learned journals and presented papers to more than 30 conferences. Since then the total has been, in both cases, zero.' Knox was no longer smiling. Collymoon's brow glowed. There were several uncomfortable minutes of silence, then Knox continued in a low, funereal tone, 'There was no book on the Scottish Reformation, Professor Collymoon, was there?'

'No.' The voice was quiet, defeated, resigned.

'You lost your love for the subject, perhaps?'

'Something like that,' said Collymoon in the faintest of voices, 'There comes a time when you look at your life's work and think, is that all there is? Researching and the words and ideas of long-dead clerics?'

'Hear, hear,' I couldn't help from exclaiming, drawing a dread stare from Knox.

'My father worked in an iron foundry,' Collymoon went on, 'He was a moulder. Products he worked on are still in situ all over the country, all over Europe, in South America, South Africa, Australia, Singapore. He and his colleagues *made* things, things that worked, things that served people. The foundry closed down thirty years ago, but their stuff still does its job. What have *I* ever done?'

Knox ignored the question. 'You were no longer able to produce the research that your post at the University requires you to do, so you conceived the idea that there was a great work in progress, and the notion of having lost it all through a fictional theft.'

This was rather rubbing it in, but Collymoon simply hung his head and gave a kind of dejected nod.

'And the pottery classes? Oh, yes, we know about them.'

'Knox, I now *make* things, too. I get my hands dirty, work with the clay, and produce things that work, that serve a purpose, that are beautiful.'

I looked at the miserable objects on display and tried to keep a straight face.

✪

'You only ever really use me as a *witness*, don't you, Knox?' I said on the journey home.

'That is a calumny, Malky. My conclusions about the case were formed while you and Gilbert made your valuable contributions to an illuminating discussion.'

'What will happen to him?'

'I do not know. He has committed no particular crime, though he has perhaps misled his employer to the extent that he could be dismissed. I have recommended that he confess the situation to his superiors and, as it were, throw himself on their mercy.'

'Well, I think he has a point. What's the point of ecclesiastical history research anyway?'

Knox shook his head with a deep and genuine sadness. 'Malky, there are times when I wonder if there is a place for someone as anti-intellectual as yourself in Higher Education.'

I had been put in my place again. I drove on into the long June twilight

---

26

Teen Spirit

Max Dunbar

Party at Matt Kingswood's! Non parental Friday night! Put an order in for 20-20, Aftershocks, Jagermeister. Johnny Wright from the other half year says he can get served at Tesco now but might as well go to News and Booze because anyone can get served there. What about reefas. Putting an order in for an ounce of weed. From Garvey in 9C. No fuck that because Garvey takes ages to score and wants to bring his brothers around (this lad Garvey knows chats you up by saying 'Hey, I've been to prison' YEAH WERE SO IMPRESSED). Need to smoke reefs outside, cant explain rockburned carpet to parentals! Music looking at Arctic Monkeys, London Grammar, Caribou, Mark Lanegan, The Coral, Prodigy, Basement Jaxx, LL Cool J, Libertines (NO ONE DIRECTION/ADELLE/ED SHEERAN!!!) Munchiefood Haribo (sourmix) Heroes, Doritos and dips. Karaoke wii and Fifa. Looking at 100 peeps coming, top boys from the year (Andy Liston/Ste Cormick/Bri Ellerby/Bagger/Tom Bob) plus FITTIES from the year, Xsection from sports teams (NOT BARBARA WATSON, SHE LOOKS LIKE A MAN) drama group and estate fanny (Rachel Yeadon/Cyenna Corliss/Ursula Hartington/Kayleigh Stamhurst/Iona McLeod) NO MINGERS – NO ONE WHO GETS 'DRUNK AND EMOTIONAL' (HAHA LYNSEY-MAE HARROW IM LOOKING AT YOU!) MAYBE SOME EMOS/MOSHERS – THE COOL ONES – SOME GEEKS ARE FIT – ANNIE BAYLISS AND THAT CROWD WHO HANG AROUND THE FOREST AT DINNER – NO SELF HARMAS!!! No one from the year above. No male geeks. PARENTALS BACK SATURDAY EVE, NEED TO TIDY AFTERWARDS, CAREFUL OF SPILLED DRINKS ON FURNITURE ETC. PARTY AT MATT

KINGSWOOD'S! NON PARENTAL 8 FRIDAY NIGHT!

Kingswood shut down the messenger function on his laptop and the Tor net explorer. It was almost evening and the sunlight had become gravid, with things floating in it. He tidied away the incriminators – weekend *Telegraph,* golfing bag, SAS memoirs – and the essentials: rope, taser, chloroform, digital camera, USB stick, A-Z with local schools, children's homes and ASB hotspots marked out in his careful highlighter. This was the house his mother had left him, it opened onto the street, with a long driveway. This had taken months to set up. He didn't mind waiting and planning. Waiting and planning were part of the buzz. Probably fewer than a dozen would come: perhaps only one or two would come. He sat on his armchair and awaited teenage laughter and the scurry of high-street heels and fashionable trainers.

Say It With Flowers

Sue Iles-Jones

None of the lads were prepared to take on the personal responsibility for the funeral, though they were determined to have a say in how Darren was to be despatched. To ensure that he was 'seen off properly' Darren's large collection of mates gave extremely specific instructions to the undertakers and florist. To achieve this, and for their own convenience, they'd chosen to use the florists which was only four doors along from the *Dog and Basket* pub, which was how Araminta of *Blooming Amazing* came to be preparing such unusual arrangements. Many of the men still clutched their pints emotionally as Araminta took down their personal requests.

The deceased had been something of a local character, whose exacting lifestyle of beer and takeaways had undoubtedly compromised his health. Though it transpired that his own last orders had in fact been called when he slipped on the steps of the pub where he so often held court, just as he was taking a fag break. Witnesses were sure that if he hadn't been so determined to keep his pint upright as his legs shot from under him, there may have been a chance that he might have been able to save his head from cracking open on the step. But that was Daz all over, they said. He would never waste beer.

The day of the funeral dawned, and in *Blooming Amazing* the floral arrangements were set out in a row towards the door of the shop waiting for the hearse to arrive. The first was a design in the shape of two beer glasses. They were made up of golden yellow chrysanthemums with a 'head' of white ones. One glass was supposed to be half drunk, and bore a card with the message '*Have one on me mate. Cheers Lee.*' The next was shaped as a pair of buttocks with the flowers sprayed a skin pink colour to achieve the required effect. A vivid red lace thong was threaded over it and attached was the note *'Bottoms Up!'* The big display was the word *'DAZZA'* spelt out in large individual flower letters, and the card said *'This lot cost me the £190 I owe you mate. The other tenner went on scratch cards. Now we're quits. All the best, from Lucky.'*

It seemed that Darren's fondness for curries was remembered with great affection, and Araminta had been asked to make a floral display that resembled a chicken tikka masala. She had baulked at the challenge this presented, and instead made a more tasteful composition using various chillies in different colours, shapes and sizes, edged with coriander leaves and interwoven with cinnamon sticks and cardamom seeds. However, she had no discretion in the setting for this arrangement, having been instructed to place it around the toilet seat from the pub, which was believed to have been the last one the deceased had sat on. The accompanying note was affixed to an Indian take away menu and which now rested on the loo seat/chilli display. Its contents contained an unarguable logic. *'No need to worry about the ring of fire now Daz. Just look out for the other one! Hard luck mate, it couldn't have happened to a nicer bloke. From all of us at the Dog and Basket.*

The door to *Blooming Amazing* opened and Araminta's undertaker colleague Funeral Frank picked his way carefully in. Araminta was at once struck by the overwhelming odour of curry emanating from his elegant but normally fragrant black suit. At the risk of offending him she had to comment, 'Goodness Frank, its not like you to smell of yesterday's dinner.'

He tossed his head, 'Don't even start love. Oh yes, I can varda all Darren's zhooshed up tributes. This is going to be a day and a half I can tell you. I can already feel it in my water. What a palaver! Would you believe this? I've had to surround him in the coffin with a take away comprising nothing less than a meat bhuna, tandoori chicken, lamb vindaloo, prawn madras not to mention a large pilau rice, chapatis, a stuffed naan, pappadoms, a portion of samosas and two onion bhajis! My instructions were to get them from his favourite curry house, which being the consummate professional that I am, I did last night so as they wouldn't heat him up, as it were. Well, I've had this greasy carrier bag and its naff smell invading my flat, car and now hearse. The coffin lid is screwed down but you can still smell it. Those foil boxes don't half leak and the sag bhaji all but exploded as I put it in.'

'You actually put a curry in with the body?' Araminta was astonished.

'Oh yes love, you stick to your bloody flowers, you've no idea of the detailed work we undertakers have to do. It isn't all overcharging for melamine coffins with plastic handles, I can tell you. So, as I said, I've had to put all this round him and naturally I spaced it out as symmetrically as I could...'

'Naturally,' she laughed.

'Its not bloody funny girl. The oil ran out of the bottom of those cheap containers and before you could say "Taj Mahal", the satin was stained orange and was greasier than the worst type of politician. I placed the onion bhajis on his testicles as it seemed right, and a piece of chapati over each eye. The lemon wedges, mint sauce and various chutney's got spaced in at intervals around his person. However, as if that wasn't enough I had to put eight cans of Stella in between his lallies as well, along with a packet of Marlboro Lights – though what difference the low tar will make now, I've no idea. I should have said 'no', really I should. I'm not getting any younger, and these 'last requests' are getting right out of hand. What's the tax office going to say when they see my invoice for the off licence and curry house? Wouldn't surprise me if we didn't get a visit from Watchdog saying we were having a laugh at the expense of the deceased.'

'Why did they want all that done?' Araminta asked, as she began helping Frank to carry the tributes out to the hearse.

'Oh, his mates are a pack of self-styled comedians, and they claimed he was part of an Egyptian cult and that he must be buried

---

31

with enough food to see him through into the afterlife. Egyptian my arse! The nearest he got to Egypt was that Moroccan boyfriend his mother had. You know that waiter from the kebab shop near the station?'

'Can't say that I do.'

'No? One of my gentlemen friends is partial to some sustenance there after a heavy night, so to speak, which is how I heard that gossip. I'm too particular to go there myself and I wouldn't let anything like that pass my lips, I can tell you.'

'Indeed not,' Araminta agreed from behind the flowery pint glasses.

'His pub mates had the cheek to ask for me to put a kebab in there too, but, no, I drew the line, and I told them that I wasn't a fast food truck. Just what's happened to tasteful send-offs I want to know? Remember when we started working together a couple of years ago? I know I came up with some wild ideas, but my "Death doesn't have to be the End," concept was supposed to be about expanding the business and commemorations and memorials - not all this old dross…'

Araminta interrupted him 'Careful as you carry out the one with the chillies, or at least wash your hands before using the toilet. You'll regret it if you don't.'

'Been there done that, my dear, and you don't make *that* mistake twice. Oh my God, was it inflamed! My boyfriend couldn't stop admiring it, but I had no choice but to stick it in a pot of yoghurt just to get some relief, as they say.'

Araminta went to pick up the flowery thong covered buttocks and began carrying them out. As she went towards the hearse, she passed a large cat basket outside the front of her shop. While putting the display next to the coffin she certainly did notice the smell of curry, so much so that she half expected to see the orangey red oil dripping out of the bottom. She also couldn't get the thought of the onion bhajis on his groin out of her head.

As she turned back to the shop she saw Frank pick up the cat basket and take it inside. It wasn't the first time that a cat had been left there, as the vet's surgery next door often ended up with abandoned animals whose owners were too mean and spineless to pay for their treatment. If the vets weren't open, *Blooming Amazing* was the nearest doorway. She saw Frank raise the basket to eye level, then by the time she reached him, he had caught the toe of one of his pointy shoes in one of the 'Z's' of the DAZZA display causing him to trip sideways. The cat basket crashed to the floor. Inside was not an abandoned feline, but a very large seagull, which was pushed against the wicker sides, filling it to capacity. Its beak even protruded through the grill, and its angry yellow eyes stared out of a ruffled head that was on one side. There was a note, which was now detached. It simply said. 'Please put me to sleep.'

Apart from being dropped by Frank, who was now in the process of picking up the chilli display, the bird looked fine.

'Probably the victim of a gull hater. Poor thing, I'll call him Gulliver – he's got every right to live,' said Araminta. She went to the door with the heavy basket. She put it on the ground and opened the grill to let it fly or hop to freedom. The bird made its way out slowly.

'Probably giddy after being dropped,' she called back to Frank.

'I said it was going to be a day and a half, and I'm never wrong,' he replied.

He wasn't. The gull stretched one leg at a time out behind him and then took to the air, but unfortunately flew straight back into the shop as it did so. Araminta ducked as it whooshed over her head, and screaming in shock. Frank looked up from the chillies, in time to see it clip him on the head and crash into the displays in its confusion and terror.

'Shoo it out girl,' yelled Frank.

'If you hadn't given it concussion, then it might have flown straight,' she retorted.

'Oh I've made it gay have I?'

'Just shut up, and help!'

The bird careered back and forth knocking into baskets and ribbons screaming and squawking.

'Araminta, if that bird does anything nasty on me, you can pay for the cleaning bill. I'm warning you…' Frank dived and hid his eyes from the bird, which was approaching. Immediately he started yelling and jumping about as the chilli from his fingers went into his eyes.

'Jesus bloody Christ, help me. I'm blinded, help me for God's sake.' He sightlessly grabbed one of the few buckets that were still standing and doused his head with its contents. Peonies and water cascaded down his black suit, leaving him looking like a 1960's hippy in a rainstorm.

'He seems to be able to fly alright, so why would anyone want to have him put to sleep?' asked Araminta almost rhetorically.

'I can think of a couple of reasons,' said Frank sobbing.

There was no choice but for Araminta to close the shop and drive the hearse, as Frank's partial sight, though temporary, rendered him a motoring liability. His eyes were so tear filled, swollen and red that Darren's shocked mates thought that he must be the chief mourner.

'Perhaps Daz was bent?' they whispered to each other at the pub afterwards. 'That undertaker queen wasn't half gutted.'

Later that afternoon back in her shop, although Araminta had to clean up the mess that Frank and Gulliver had created, she happily reflected on the admiration her displays had received at the funeral. True their imagery was unusual but it seemed that people liked her creative style and many had made a note of her details for the future. It was universally hard to find the right words to express feelings at sad times and flowers really did say it all.

Ever since Araminta had the idea of working with Frank's undertaker's emporium *Happy Endings* she had gone to some considerable effort to ensure that there was an steady flow of lucrative funeral work and with her careful planning, despite the

—

recession, business was indeed blooming amazing.

Before she locked up, she once again popped a clear bottle of glycerine into her handbag. It was typically used to preserve flowers and leaves, but was treacherously slippery and if spilt could cause all manner of nasty if not fatal accidents particularly if anyone walked on it. Araminta knew that nothing was ever certain, but as Darren would testify if he were here, it's is pretty hard to keep your balance once you are on it. Tonight, by way of a change, Araminta had set her sights on the disabled ramp outside the church hall, which she felt offered definite possibilities. Closing the door behind her, she set off there with a sense of speed and purpose, as she knew that the stroke club would be emerging in half an hour.

Fresh Fish

Christopher P. Mooney

I awake from the fleeting respite of a soon-distant dream to the living nightmare of my windowless cell. There are no features or fittings of any kind in here. No sink, no bed and not even a toilet. I haven't left the confines of this cramped space since I was marched in here by a squad of officers, my handcuffs and ankle shackles fastened too tightly to a metal chain around my waist. I estimate that to be about four or five days ago but it is impossible to know for sure. There seems to be no routine to speak of. There is no light, no air and no view. Except for the hand in the slot three times a day and, of course, the beating, absolutely no human contact. The so-called meals never change so I can't even tell the time of day by what the hand delivers.

The cold concrete floor chills my naked skin, which is marked with purple bruises and dried blood from last night's beating by the prison officials. I am disgusted to notice that my bare crotch and legs are damp with my own urine. I am ashamed that my backside, my back and the backs of my legs are caked with a thick layer of my own feces.

I cannot believe that I have sunk so low, so quickly.

The flap at the bottom of the enormous door opens and closes, all of it done in the time it takes for a sweaty hand to thrust through what passes for a meal here. A bread roll and a banana. Nothing else. The roll is encrusted with a blue-green mold. The skin of the banana is black. I devour all of it in only a few minutes.

I can hear the guard's footsteps as he paces the block, delivering this feast to the other prisoners who are locked behind the door in what I assume are cells identical to my own. I can't see them

36

but I hear some of them at night. Their wild shouts, their maniacal screams. Their threats and curses and protestations. The hoarse, agonizing sobs of those who cry themselves to sleep. The primal noises of men who have been reduced to mere beasts.

My throat is dry. Against my better judgment, I bang on the door with my clenched fists. I get down on my knees and shout a request for a cup of water through the flap. It was a more extreme episode of this kind of behavior that earned me the bruises. Predictably, there is no response. I console myself with the fact that at least this time they don't come in mob-handed and kick my head in.

Welcome to solitary. Welcome to Hell.

With nothing to do but wait, I lie on my back on the ground, in the dark, hopefully in a spot without feces. My mind and body, having been inactive and unstimulated for so long, need no invitation to shut down and drift back to the shelter of meaningless sleep.

✪

I hear the bolts being moved aside and the keys being turned in the locks. The door is open before I can get to my feet. A uniformed officer with a baby face, certainly at least half of my fifty-two years and probably quite new to the job, is standing in the doorframe. Is this the owner of the hand that feeds me?

Babyface throws a tattered, bright-orange jumpsuit into the cell.

'Put that on and hurry up about it. I haven't got all day.'

The jumpsuit has DEPARTMENT OF CORRECTIONS written in black letters across the chest, across the back and down the outside of both legs, and it smells almost as bad as I do. Babyface trusses me up as before with the collection of chains and cuffs and then marches me out of the cell, along the corridor, through another heavily-bolted door and finally, mercifully, out of the solitary block. To this day, I am convinced that some of my soul

—

and a significant portion of my dignity are still there.

Outside of the solitary block and in some sort of holding area, I come face to face with half a dozen other inmates, all of whom obviously share my taste in clothes. Three of them are white and three of them are black. The white guys are seated on one bench, which is really nothing more than a horizontal concrete slab bolted crudely to a wall, at one side of the room and the black guys are seated on an identical bench at the other side of the room.

'Sit down, convict,' yells Babyface.

I have a split second to make my decision, which is really no decision at all. Although I've been down for only a short time, I've nonetheless picked up enough to know that in this system whites stick with whites and blacks stick with blacks. I usually try my best to get along with everybody and the color of a man's skin makes no difference to me, but I know that this is neither the time nor the place to make any kind of statement.

Watched all the way by every eye in the place, I shuffle over and sit with the other white-skinned convicts. I have made my choice and in doing so have aligned myself with some convicts and alienated myself from some others. In more general terms, this is the nature of the beast.

White skin seems to be the only thing that I have in common with these people. For starters, I am the only person on our bench with a full set of teeth. My hair is cropped, short and tidy; two of them have hair that is overly long and greasy and is matted to their foreheads. I do not have tattoos on my neck or hands. All of the others do. One of them even has a tattoo on his face. Think small-town hicks. Think trailer parks. Think bad breeding and bestiality. The thought of spending the next decade of my life with these people, and with others like them, makes my stomach churn.

The largest of these, whose name is given as Bones, is quite possibly the biggest person I have ever seen. His ink-covered frame is an enormous mass of pure muscle. Even his fingers seem abnormally large. I wonder to myself if this makes it more difficult

—

for him to pluck the strings of his banjo. Unlike the other two, Bones does not have horrible hair. He doesn't have any hair at all. Also, most of his teeth, although quite yellow, are still in place.

Bones and the other two white guys glare menacingly at the black guys on the other side. The black guys, for their part, glare right back.

Bones is the first to break the silence.

'Hey, fresh fish.'

A fish, of course, is a person who is experiencing the delights of prison life for the very first time. Bones and I have never met before and therefore he really has no idea as to who I am or what I am in for, nor does he know if I have ever previously been incarcerated, but he can probably tell that I'm new to this form of housing arrangement by way of a thousand indicators that I am involuntarily giving off and am utterly unaware of. Or maybe he can simply see from my face that I am terribly frightened.

'Hey, fresh fish,' he says again.

Either way, he is definitely talking to me.

I try my best not to be intimidated or to show any fear as I look this man-mountain in the eyes via an upward trajectory.

'Can I help you?' I reply.

Fuck. Why did I say that?

'No, you can't help me, you fresh fish motherfucker. You think you're better than me? You can't be helpin' Bones with shit.'

'I'm sorry, I….'

'You will be sorry, fish. Now be a good boy and tell us how come you ended up with them there bruises.'

This time I look at my feet, via a downward trajectory, and when I speak I am less careful about my pronunciation:

'The officers in solitary filled me in good 'cause I repeatedly asked for a glass of water.'

It's as if a bomb has gone off. The revelation that my bruised appearance is a result of officer violence sets off both benches.

'Whaaat! That be some fucked up shit, dawg,' says

Deliverance Number One on my bench.

'Them punk-ass bitches be trippin',' says Deliverance Number Two.

The black prisoners on the other bench are equally appalled and join in. For a brief moment, we are all united. Apparently news of a fellow con being tuned up by the guards is enough to achieve racial solidarity, if only for a moment.

'White boy be busted for asking for a glass of water. That's off the hook, y'all.'

A second question from Bones quells the protests.

'Did you snitch, though?'

His tone is accusatory. The atmosphere is suddenly tense. There is absolute silence as everyone waits for my answer.

At this point, my knowledge of being incarcerated is, admittedly, very limited. However, I have enough about me to know that you never, ever snitch; even on over-zealous custodians. It is the ultimate no-no. In prison, snitches get stitches. Grasses, rats, stoolies, snakes, chivatos, have a remarkably short life expectancy. They rarely die peacefully in their bunks and are usually awarded the same underclass status as rapists and child molesters.

Therefore, I open my mouth very slowly and choose my words very carefully.

'Nah, I'm not down with that,' I say. 'When they asked, I told them that I had slipped over in the cell. I told them that it was my own fault and that nobody else was involved.'

To be fair, this was exactly what I did tell the prison official who had enquired about my injuries and the prison doctor who had treated them. They both gave me quizzical looks but neither of them chose to press the issue.

'Good for you, dawg,' Deliverance Number One again. 'You best be keepin' your mouth shut around here.'

'That right,' adds Bones, 'For those that don't.... Well, it ain't nuthin' nice.'

These pearls of wisdom are met with low growls and nods of

approval. Then each bench returns to its respective chatter and malevolent stares and I am left alone with my thoughts, no longer of interest.

✪

Hours pass. We, the cons, sit idly on the benches as they, the guards, busy themselves with coffee cups and magazines.

One of the guards, whose name tag reads JOHNSON, finally gets up and sees fit to address us.

'Ease forward on the bench and then drop to your knees.'

This instruction is much easier to give than it is to carry out, especially when your hands are cuffed and shackled together. Somehow, we all manage it without eating mouthfuls of concrete.

'I am now going to uncuff you,' continues Johnson, 'and as soon as I do, put your hands on your heads. Any other movement will be considered as a movement of aggression and I will take the chance to blow your fucking brains out.'

There is no way to know if he means it or not but I, for one, have no intention of finding out. As soon as my cuffs have been removed, I put the palms of my hands on top of my head and I make sure that I don't even twitch.

'Now, when your name is called, you stand up and move slowly over to the counter. There you will be provided with standard prison issue. Any sudden movements, any comments, any bullshit whatsoever, and I swear to Jesus Christ that I will end you.'

My name is the last to be called. After struggling to my feet, I proceed to the counter, where I am issued with my new – well, new to me – worldly possessions. One blue jumpsuit, one pair of socks, one pair of underpants, one pair of plastic shoes and one pair of plastic shower sandals. Everything is second-hand, everything is stained, and everything seems to stink of urine. Habit and reflex cause me to say thank you for my bundle but I am anything but grateful.

I am then shown into a side room where a young guard

brusquely orders me to strip.

'All the way?' I ask.

'That's right, convict. All you should be wearing is your birthday suit. Now strip.'

I remove my civilian clothes and stand before him, completely naked and vulnerable.

'Only do what I tell you to do, when I tell you to do it. Is that understood?'

'Yes, understood.'

'Lift your arms up and out to the sides... Open the palms and extend the fingers... Use the tips of your fingers to push your ears forward... Run your hands through your hair... Put your arms down by your sides... Open your mouth and extend your tongue... Turn around... Lift up your left leg and show me the sole of your left foot... Now lift your right leg and show me the sole of your right foot... Bend over and touch your toes... Use your hands to pull apart your ass cheeks... Cough... Again... Now stand up straight... Turn back around... Lift up your balls... Peel back your foreskin... Ok, you're clean. You can put on your prison issue.'

As soon as the jumpsuit is on, I am handcuffed and the cuffs are again shackled to my waist. I join the others in the back of a prison van, where our belly chains are hooked together and then fastened to bolts in the floor. The van's engine coughs and splutters into action and the van jolts forward, causing all of us to lose our balance and fall helplessly against each other. Then we are on our way and I know it ain't gonna be nuthin' nice. Destination: Federal Penitentiary. The beginning of the end of my life as I know it.

Not Home

Sleiman El Hajj

A woman wearing a black velvet jacket and mauve slippers came through the lobby door walking a kitten on a tiny leash and stood beside me as I waited for the elevator. I remembered a documentary I'd watched on television about how cats could learn to walk in harnesses if the training were done at an early age. Clearly, the woman knew what she was doing. She seemed middle-aged, but it was hard to tell.

This was the second day of my stay in London, and I had just had a glass of chilled mineral water to calm my nerves. The news from home was distressing: suicide bombings were multiplying by the day, as if by binary fission. Southern Beirut was no longer home.

The elevator door finally opened, and the woman, the kitten, and I got in. The woman picked her up and pushed her floor button with the creature's small paw.

Later that evening, the same woman followed closely by a lanky man who looked half her age and seemed to be carrying the kitten grudgingly, spotted me looking at her from across the lobby. This was the only part of the three-star hotel that had wireless connection; I was trying to decide what do with my backlog of home email, willing myself to look away from the laptop for a moment.

The woman, followed by the man, walked over uninvited. 'Do you see this man behind me?' the woman said. 'I'm his boss, and he wants to fuck me. Else, he will tell police what he saw that morning, and they'll take the cat away!' She waved her hands helplessly, expecting a response.

'Why are you telling me this?' I asked icily, adjusting my veil.

The woman looked at me, surprised and reproachful. 'I'm already three sheets into the wind,' she explained. "And your face looked familiar.'

'Come," she said to the man shifting restlessly behind her, the cat held forward in the crook of his hands. "Let's get this done.'

A Moment in Time

Kat Williams

'Nick Sinclair?'

His attention is taken away from his first important decision of the day - scrambled or poached? The microwave opposite displays the digits 07:05. Sinclair's impressed; he's managed a personal best with his five mile run.

He cradles his mobile between his shoulder and cheek.

'Well, that depends. Are you attractive, single and looking for some company in your life?' he replies.

The woman manages a strained laugh.

'Hell, you don't *even* have to be single, I won't tell anyone,' Sinclair winks at his own reflection in the microwave.'In fact, I'm free tonight...'

'I'd hate to turn you down on such an offer,' she answers, her voice sounding further away, 'but I won't be around tonight.'

'Well, I could wait 'till you were back but I don't even know what you look like. And for me to commit to something on that basis... well, Sweetheart, it just isn't my style.' He places his phone on the counter and turns on the loud speaker. Sinclair pulls open the fridge. His fingers drum on the open door.

'Well, it's difficult circumstances.'

'I see...' he nods at the fridge.

'I've been... murdered.'

Her voice echoes around the kitchen. It bounces off every surface. Sinclair drops the eggs. They fire and explode like grenades as they impact on the tiles. A massacre-like mess is left with the burnt orange yolks stark against the black.

'Sinclair?'

It's been a long time since a female has left Sinclair speechless.

'I'm still here.'

The woman continues, 'I'm going to help you find my killer.'

The toaster pops. Heat radiates up, slowly, casually and unnoticed. The slices of toast were late to the party. Sinclair is already out the door.

✪

The pedal's to the floor. The streets are barely waking up. Only flickers of life are visible. Everyone is sleeping soundly unaware of a murder being committed right this moment, while they dream. It's 07:13.

Eight minutes have flashed by since his mobile phone rung. Five minutes and twenty-five seconds has passed since he jumped into his car. And four minutes and fifteen-seconds has gone by since he'd called Taylor and told him to get his arse out of bed; he'd be there before Taylor could zip up his fly.

The tyres squeal and shriek on the tarmac. He pulls up outside the terraced house with the angry red front door. He thumps the steering wheel and the horn blasts out.

Seconds pass, Sinclair glances at his watch. Time is imperative today.

He punches the steering wheel again harder and longer. The door opens and Taylor rushes out still fastening the last few buttons on his shirt. He jerks open the car door.

The car is pulling away from the curb before Taylor has even got his left leg in.

'Easy, Sinclair.'

Sinclair shoots a question towards him, 'Have you contacted the station? Called an Ambulance?'

'Ambulance is on its way. They've also received a call from the woman's colleague only 5 minutes ago.'

'Huh. What took them so long to call?' Sinclair jumps the lights.

'Only just got into work,' answers Taylor. He looks across at Sinclair. 'Your hands, they're shaking.'

'Missed that first espresso of the day. Anyway, back to what's important.'

Taylor frowns. 'Took a while to make sense of the bloke. You probably got more out of the living, breathing dead victim.' He pauses. 'Anything else I need to know?'

'No more than what I've already told you.' Sinclair steals a glance at his watch, thirty seconds past 07:23. 'Name is Karen Ellis. She's a specialist in chemical and biological poisons, viruses, that sort of thing. She'd been to a conference, which lasted a couple of hours, then a handful of them moved on to grab some food and then onto a local bar. There, she felt ill.'

'One too many?'

'She didn't seem to think so. She said that she knew something wasn't right. Went to her car, used a kit that she transports from work to home, took some of her own blood...'

Taylor squirms. Sixteen years on the job and there were still things that gave him the feeling of someone dancing on his grave.

Sinclair swerves as the car taking a hair pin corner down a back alley.

He continues, 'took her own blood; did some basic tests; saw something that shouldn't have been there; did it again; same result. She ends up driving herself to her office in the lab, twenty minutes away.'

'What time was all that?' asks Taylor.

'Conference ended late; question time ran over; they got out at 10; went to a late night restaurant for food; restaurant chucked them out at 11:15; moved to a bar where she felt ill and left at 12:30. Then walked to the car, took her own blood tests, drove to her lab where she took more tests. She sets an alarm for when she would have her results and waited. It all clocks up.'

Taylor nods. 'Anything else?'

'You should be grateful that I got that much out of her. We really are running to the wire if what she says is true...'

'We need to get the most out of her while she's still...' Taylor's voice trails off.

Sinclair slams on and Taylor lurches forward. They had arrived. There is no ambulance in sight.

The sun is rising behind Karen Ellis' work building. It was going to be a glorious day. Nothing stopped the weather. Not even a murder.

✪

Sinclair and Taylor are hurried along the corridors, at the speed of a rabbit being chased at the dog races. They can feel the dog's breath hot on their necks. Karen Ellis' skinny, adolescent-looking colleague is obviously affected by what he has walked into that morning. He stutters every time he speaks and only manages to force a few muffled words to Taylor and Sinclair.

They head to the front of the clinical looking building where the assistant struggles to swipe his ID card. Sinclair snatches the plastic card from him, swiping it in the machine before placing it within the pocket of the young man's lab coat. He wears a name tag.

'Thanks, Sam,' Sinclair says.

They follow corridor after corridor, each one as identical as the last. The flooring whiter than bone, the walls even whiter.

'She's in here,' the colleague finally says as they enter a large lab.

Sinclair is moments away from seeing his victim. There would be no white suits, no post mortem and no body. Not yet anyway. But somewhere there was a murderer.

Sinclair instructs Taylor to speak to Sam and the other colleagues. He walks over to the only other person in the lab.

Karen Ellis is sitting in front of a computer. Her skin has a bluish tint to it. As he comes closer, she looks up. Her pupils are dilated but she looks relatively alert. There's a sheen of sweat on her forehead. Her make up is sliding down her face reminding him of the mess he left on the kitchen floor.

She goes to stand. It's slow and awkward for someone who looks to be no older than thirty; the desk is her crutch. From out of the glow of the computer, he realises that her skin is actually blue as though it is her natural colour. But it isn't natural. Her lips are disappearing, a grey merging with the blue. Is she freezing to death from the inside-out? She's wearing a lab coat, making her look like one of Dracula's brides.

She reaches out a hand to Sinclair. Her grasp surprises him; it's cold but firm. Shaking a dead person's hand, he thinks, never done that before.

'Thanks… for coming,' she says through gasps, greeting him as though she had invited Sinclair round to a celebratory occasion. 'I didn't… know who… else to call…' Her breathing is a struggle, like an air being slowly squeezed out of a balloon.

'Save your energy,' he says and motions for her to sit back down. He's shocked at how in only thirty-six minutes Karen Ellis has deteriorated so quickly.

She barely nods but follows his instruction.

'I don't have much… time,' Karen swallows. 'The poison… it's something we've… been working on…'

'Is this what you think you have?'

Sinclair waits for her to answer, watching as Sam leads Taylor out of the room.

'I know it is,' Karen Ellis wheezes.

Sinclair pushes a glass of water towards her. Her hands shake. The control of her limbs is no longer up to her. She is her body's own puppet.

'It's a nerve agent called Sarin… most know it as… a biological weapon but… we made discoveries… ones that could help... the medical practice... We were in the early stages of...' She clutches a tissue, dabbing her nose. 'We hadn't tried it on humans,' she says. 'It's deadly... in its raw form.'

She manages a wheezy laugh, which sounds more like a squeaky toy with no squeak left. A few precious moments pass as she struggles for breath. 'We do have... samples of Sarin... It's a colourless liquid... no odour... You can either inhale... or absorb it.'

'Locked away? Limited access?'

She nods. Then swallows.

'How would they have gained access to it?'

'It's someone who works here... They know where... it's stored...The security code...'

'Have you checked the supplies?'

'There's some missing.'

'How much?'

'Enough... to kill me before we finish... our conversation.' She grimaces.

Sinclair can't work out if Karen Ellis is being morbidly sarcastic or preparing them both for what will happen. She places a hand upon her chest as though restraining herself from being sick. Her eyes close.

Another glance at his watch; 07:55.

Karen Ellis manages to compose herself. She pushes a piece of paper across the desk to Sinclair. 'Here's what I know... that could help you...'

She moves her finger down a list of clinical staff, stopping part way down. Her finger lingers, her nail the colour of raw fish. 'This is my killer.'

'How do you know that it is this Caroline Krest?' Sinclair says as he scans the rest of the list.

'Because you and me have... something in common... we have enemies, Nick Sinclair. We do things... people get hurt... we move on...'

She gasps for breath. She's drowning.

—

She chokes out, 'This wasn't what I wanted… She wouldn't accept it… told me that if she couldn't have me… no-one—'

Karen Ellis' body starts to jerk. She's falling from her desk chair. Sinclair catches her head before she hits the floor. Traces of his earlier tremors are still present in his hands. He shouts out but no-one comes. He can't reach his mobile and he doesn't want to let go of her.

Drool leaks from the corner of her mouth like a fresh wound and her eyelids flutter. Her shoes clack against the tiles enacting a morbid foxtrot. Time finally slows for Sinclair, but it's too late.

The movement from beneath his hands subsides. He listens for her laboured breathing. There is none. Placing her head down he takes her wrist and checks her pulse. He holds it longer than he needs to. Eventually, he drops it.

Taylor rounds the corner, 'we should have...' He stops when he sees the scene in front of him.

Less than an hour has passed since Karen Ellis had entered Sinclair's life. Now she's gone already.

✪

Standing outside, they pinpoint Karen Ellis' car. Sinclair holds the keys.

An ambulance turns in. Sinclair glares at it as it flaunts its noise and lights. Two paramedics jump out.

'You're as much use a toy soldiers,' Sinclair barks. 'You're too late. We need pathologists not paramedics.'

They look at Taylor who shrugs his shoulders and watches them head into the building.

Sinclair tuts.

'So this Caroline Krest, does have a motive,' Taylor begins. Sinclair had already filled Taylor in with what he had learnt, showing him the printed list of names. 'If you class having an affair with your *female* colleague, who leaves their…'

'Civil partnership.'

'Civil partnership of seven years, to be with their 'mistress' who they work with. Ellis flaunts in, sleeps with Krest, woos her and then when Ellis gets what she wants, drops Krest like a piece of dirty washing. I'd be pissed.'

'It's happened to you before.'

Taylor ignores his remark. 'Ellis wanted to sample and when it wasn't what she thought it was, she wanted her money back. Ellis didn't want Krest. Clearly Krest couldn't deal with it.'

'Now that's covered, Taylor, in as much detail as you could muster, we need to find out, how?'

'So, it's either inhalation or absorption, right?'

'Uhuh,' Sinclair answers. 'The effects happened very quickly. Did Krest mean to kill her or just poison her?'

'Well, I was told that there *is* a cure if it's taken within a certain amount of time after exposure. It's only a small window, less than an hour and obviously she missed it. Sam did say it happened quicker than usual; higher concentration.'

Karen Ellis' final moments burned in Sinclair's mind.

'Let's get started,' says Sinclair,

Taylor takes the boot of the car. Sinclair searches the front. He does the usual checkpoints; the glove compartment, the visors, behind and under the seats and the side of the doors.

Nothing.

Her car is immaculately tidy. Nothing is out of place. There is no loose change, no spare jacket or rubbish. It's like the car had just been driven out of the show room. The only hint of a personality is an air freshener poised on one of the air vents.

Sinclair sniffs. Funny, there isn't even a hint of a smell in the car. Not the vanilla essence that the label on the air freshener claims to be.

What did Karen Ellis say about this Sarin?

'It's a colourless liquid… no odour… and you can either inhale… or absorb it.'

What if you were exposed to it without even realising it? What if Karen Ellis unknowingly walked into her own death trap? She felt unwell; maybe it was just a bad bit of food. She sits in her car. She's in close contact with Sarin the whole time. It would have penetrated every inch of her body, inside and out as easy as a sponge absorbing water. By the time she reaches the lab, the damage is done.

The poison has been in plain sight the whole time.

'Jesus Christ.' He jumps out of the car. His watch beeps. It's 08:37 and he's just found the murder weapon. It's time for that white suit, and ideally, a respirator too.

Something to Keep You Warm

J. David Jaggers

Jesse sat on the curb with his back to the biting January wind. The cardboard sign that read 'Anything will help, God bless,' fluttered in his lap. A steady stream of cars and trucks pulled up and stopped at the intersection, but few made any eye contact with him. Even fewer took the trouble to roll down their window, letting in the cold to toss him a buck or some spare change. The hard faces and looks of disgust didn't bother Jesse though. Under his thick, ratty beard was a faint smile. A smile that said he had over fifty grand in the bank, and a two story brick near the park. A smile that reflected the certainty that no matter what happened to him, his daughter Zoe would continue to get his military pension.

Jesse Blackburn wasn't homeless because he had PTSD or a drug problem. Jesse was on the streets because he was looking for someone. He was hunting; hunting the fucking gutter junkie that killed his wife for the contents of her purse. Fifty dollars and a maxed-out credit card. The Marines had taught Jesse how to infiltrate and assimilate a foreign culture in order to get close to the enemy. This is what he did now, waiting and watching for his chance.

The sun began to sink behind the concrete bulk of the over-pass and the city's shadow residents started their collective migration to warmer environs. Jesse kept his seat and scanned the various ragged denizens as they shuffled past him toward the homeless shelter down on 14th. He watched them closely, looking for the crescent shape scar over a right eye. It was the last thing Sarah had said before she died. She even traced it on his face with a weak, trembling hand. Jesse took it as a last request, even though he knew she'd disapprove of his vengeance. She wanted him to be with Zoe, but he couldn't let it go. Zoe was safe with her grandmother, a woman who did appreciate his skills and the need to use them.

'You find the bastard and make him pay for my daughter's life,' she had said on that day four months ago. He had kissed Zoe and told her he was leaving for another deployment. It wasn't a hard story to believe. She protested, but even at such a young age, she knew that determined look in his eyes. He told her that he would be home soon, and for good this time. He meant it, this was his last mission.

'Damn Jay bone! It's colder than a witch's titty out here. You gonna freeze yo gonads off my man. Ha!' said a frail old black man in a big green army jacket and boots with no laces. 'You need to get on down to the center. They havin' chilli tonight my brother.'

'You know I don't do crowds JT. I got enough for a couple of pints so I'm gonna hit up the booze shop and see what kind of trouble I can get into downtown.'

'Ha, you young dudes got the skin for this cold. I can't do it no more. An old man like me needs a hot woman and some whiskey to heat up these bones Ha.'

Jesse pulled a five out of his pocket and handed it to the old man. 'Well I can't help you with the woman, but this oughta get the whiskey.'

'Bless you Jay bone. You alright for a white man.' JT slapped Jesse on the shoulder and shuffled on, his future brightened by the prospect of a pint of fire water.

There weren't any new faces on the street, so Jesse decided to move down to the bridge near the financial district. He had asked around and knew that the scar faced man went by the street name *Big Ceese*. Apparently he liked to move around a lot, mostly down to Florida, but he always came back to the city after a while. Word was that he had been banned from all of the missions for fighting, so if Jesse was going to find him, it would be out in the cold, dark night.

The underbelly of the Broad Street Bridge was mostly deserted due to the cold. There were a few dark figures huddled around a rusty barrel, an orange flame licking at its inner edge. Jesse walked up and the group parted enough for him to get a slice of the warmth. There were three of them standing around, silently staring into the barrel, their faces underlit by the flickering fire. Jesse pulled out the fresh pint of Evan Williams and passed it around without a word. It was the unspoken price for his share of the heat. One of the guys, wearing a ratty LL Bean jacket crusted with filth flashed his three existing teeth in a gnarled smile.

''Preciate it my man. This cold is somethin' fierce tonight.'

Jesse just smiled and took a swig when the bottle came back around. On the third pass, a spark popped in the piece of pallet wood burning in the barrel, and in the flash of yellow light, Jesse saw it. A thin white line like a crescent moon over the right eye of the man across from him. He felt Sarah's finger tracing it on his face and his hands automatically balled into fists. The man to Jesse's right, bundled in a thin jacket made for better weather, stuck out his gloved hand.

'Thanks for the heat brother. Name's Nig. These here are my travellin' partners Tooth and Big Ceese.'

Jesse reached out and shook Nig's hand. He didn't take his eyes off the scar faced man.

'Why you eyeballin' me prick? You wanna fuck me our somethin'?' Big Ceese said.

Jesse contained his rage and remembered his training. 'Sorry, I thought I knew you from somewhere, but I was wrong.'

Big Ceese poked a thick finger into Jesse's chest. 'Fuckin A you were wrong. You're lucky I don't break you up.'

Jesse took a breath and let the memories of his years of combat flow into his mind. He reached up and twisted the finger on his chest until it snapped. Big Ceese screamed and jerked his hand back. Jesse shot out his right hand and punched Nig in the throat. Jesse dropped down, pulled the strider blade from his boot and thrust it into Tooth's knee cap. The two men fell back on the ground at the same time screaming in pain. Big Ceese, holding his broken finger, stumbled backwards, eyes wide with fear. He turned and ran deeper under the bridge into a group of cardboard boxes used for shelter in warmer weather.

Jesse calmly wiped the blade on his leg and looked down at the two wounded men. Nig was on his knees gasping for air, oblivious to anything around him but sucking oxygen. Tooth was clutched his leg with one hand and scooted back across the gravel lot with the other. 'Don't hurt me man. I ain't wantin' no trouble.'

Jesse pointed the knife at him. 'Get out of here and you won't get any.' Tooth hobbled to his feet and took off into the cold darkness. Jesse focused his breathing and calmly started walking toward the shadows under the bridge. His senses were as sharp as they ever were in the desert, and he could hear the scar faced man's labored breathing as he tried to hide among the damp soaked cardboard.

Jesse stepped into the shadows and spoke. 'You remember that night six months ago when you stabbed a girl in the stomach with a tire iron. You took her purse,' Jesse could hear more shuffling and heavy breathing. His radar was narrowing the search.

'The bitch asked for it. She tried to spray me with some of that pepper shit. I let her have it good,' said a voice in the dark.

Jesse homed in on the voice. 'Fifty dollars. You killed her for fifty fucking dollars.' Jesse started kicking the cardboard as he closed in on the scar faced man.

'Who the fuck are you? Why do you care about some dead bitch?'

Jesse kicked a large refrigerator box to one side and found Big Ceese on his knees, the hand with the broken finger curled up on his chest. 'She was my wife. The mother of my six year old daughter.'

Big Ceese's eyes were wide with panic, and Jesse could see the glint of something metal in his other hand. He had the look of a cornered animal, and Jesse could smell the fear coming off of him.

'Fuck that bitch, and fuck you. I ain't sorry I did it.' He

57

lunged at Jesse with a thin scrap of sheet metal. Jesse stepped to the side, and kicked the man in the jaw with his boot, sending him sprawling in the gravel. Jesse swiftly came down on the man, plunging the strider blade into his exposed thigh. Blood began to flow quickly, showing black in the dim light.

'The pain you're feeling right now, that's nothing like what she had to go through. But don't worry, I'm not going to let you bleed out. That's too good for you.'

Jesse pulled a small bottle of lighter fluid from his jacket and doused the scar faced man with it. 'It's cold out here Ceese. I would hate for you to have to sleep without something to keep you warm.'

'NO! NO! I'm sorry!'

Jesse lit a match and tossed it down on the scar faced man's writhing body. The flames lit up the underside of the bridge and Jesse could see all the graffiti illuminated. He briefly warmed his hands over the fire and then headed out into the dark for home, and his daughter.

Clean

Helen Morris

She enjoys the ritual of washing up. The squirt of bright green fairy liquid, lying glutinous in the white sink. The cold and hot taps both turned on together. The rushing noise of it! The excitement. Mixing their streams to produce water so hot it has deadened the nerves in her fingers over the 50 years she's been doing it. Not that she cares. Glasses first. Two. Slowly sliding downwards into the caress of the water. A single bubble escaping. A bid for freedom, rising slowly and impossibly in an air current heated by the washing up water. She picks up her WI Birds of Britain tea towel and wafts it skywards. The rainbow pattern scrolling round as it spins slowly catching the light. She stands transfixed for a second at the motion. Before turning back to the sink. Cutlery in the bottom to soak. Two knives. Two forks. Plates. Smooth like sea shells. Two of those. The pans and trays. Two of each. Good ones. They come clean easily. She hums. No particular tune. A rolling, occupied hum of contentment. Last, the heavy marble rolling pin that had been her grandmother's. As she put it into the sink, red blooms through the water and a few sinewy, soft globules of tissue lift away, rolling, unfurling, their tendrils, gracefully reaching out. She scrubs the rest off, the bits that have stuck, efficiently, with the washing up brush. Just one. Just one rolling pin. Clean.

The single bubble floats gently downwards and settles softly just where the white bone of his skull juts into the red laval flow of the blood.

happy new year

morgan downie

they weren't certain, not at first,
what her gender was.
she'd tried to protect herself
but her splintered arms
were no shield against such rage.
it was only when they pulled
the blanket back
and found the raping
that they could be sure.

she was still alive,
in the technical sense,
so they brought her back
and we worked on her
until she wasn't.

happy new year, we said
and tried not to think
of the nameless woman
tagged and bagged, in the
mortuary fridge, throwing
back the drink, telling stories
of christmas past, forcing
our laughter, before fingering
our way back into our lives

the killing
morgan downie

we did not know what
they had beaten you with,
speculation was a television,
an unusual choice, even for us.
top to toe we document
the imprint of boots and fists,
note the power cable's dual
use as lash and ligature.

an easy intubation,
we attempt to add breath
to that last wasteland gasp
where you were dumped,
our fingers curved around
your head, your smashed
skull, fingers dipped into
the softness of brain.

the c.i.d want a cordon around you,
which i will not allow.
their flank of boyish constables,
too young yet for their cases
to be fingerprinted upon them,
could be indistinguishable from you
were it not for the uniforms
and the wreck of your face.

as they summarise your brief
but colourful charge sheet
i wonder at you as a boy,
somewhere out in parkland
beneath the clear blue
of summer sky,
all the world beautiful
and unimaginable.

A Tale of Two Claires

Alyson Lawson

It was 8.30am on the second day of the Commonwealth Games. The city was at a standstill. Claire Mitchell tried to wait patiently, wishing she was important enough to have a siren in her car. She reconsidered her passionate defence of 'The Games' to one of the more sceptical members of the force the previous day. 'Bloody, Commonwealth Games,' he'd declared. The same phrase crossed her mind now. But she shook it off, aware of how easily she could become one of *them*.

It was one of *them* who greeted her when she finally arrived at the scene. 'Mitchell, you're late. Were you washing your hair and ingesting your heart-healthy muesli?' He just needed a roll and sausage and a fag to complete the stereotype. She opened her mouth to conjure up some feminist put down but before she managed it McKay was back with, 'Doesnae matter anyway. It's probably a suicide. And remember you're just here cause the rest are on table tennis crowd management.'

If she was the star of a crime drama, Claire Mitchell would have been the fresh new Detective Constable. She'd be initially cowed by the chauvinistic cynicism of DS McKay but she'd soon break that barrier down and prove herself to be dedicated and intelligent. After a few errors, committed out of a fervent desire to do the right thing (rather than blindly follow procedure), she would have earned his respect and trust. When her affair was uncovered with the dashing but damaged Detective Inspector (*insert intimidating but sexy sounding surname*) she would at first be shunned by her colleagues. It would seem like she had thrown away all the respect gained over the course of the season. But finally in the season finale she would prove herself in some dynamic way and she would be whole-heartedly accepted, dirty affair and all.

However, Claire was living in about episode sixteen at the moment and there hadn't been much plot or character development since the pilot. Not even sex could rescue her, unless she wanted to switch sides and carry out a passionate affair with Linda Davidson their lesbian DI.

'McKay, Mitchell,' Davidson summoned them to the water's edge.

Unusually the sun had shone on Glasgow for five long days. The Clyde shimmered like tinfoil in the morning sun. The Scotstoun shipyard loomed at the opposite side – the mouth of the building shed gaping and empty. On their bank a shopping centre made of sheet metal loomed, casting an ugly shadow over the body.

The girl lay face down in the river, in black trousers and a red top, caught up in weeds near the bank. Her fair hair was strewn out on the surface and her head hung down in the water.

They were standing on the walkway beside the river. It was all part of the regeneration of the Clyde. However, this morning someone's sunny stroll or jog had been interrupted and while the diving team were about to retrieve the body a small crowd of onlookers had gathered as well. They were mostly curious dog walkers, standing on tiptoes, restraining their dogs and peering over the police line with exaggerated concern.

Suddenly from the back of the crowd they heard, 'Has there been a murder?' The dog walkers tutted and heads turned to spotlight two teenagers.

'Fuck's sake. Are they no a bit young fir Taggart?' said McKay.

'I blame ITV 4,' said Davidson. Claire laughed right on cue.

'Get rid of them McKay,' instructed Davidson. Then she turned to Claire, 'Right Mitchell, think you can cope with him for the day?' Claire nodded, a bit too eagerly. 'We want this to be as discrete as possible. At least it was a local that found her and not some tourist. Or worst still a member of the Canadian gymnastics team. At least she's washed up down-stream a bit, eh? Could be a suicide.' she said hopefully.

But when the body was finally winched out and the corpse lay on the mortuary ambulance bed, it was clear. The girl wore a necklace of blue bruises and what must have been long blonde hair, like Claire's, lay limp against her skull. Her glassy eyes stared back like one of the shopping centre mannequins.

It was clear from the lack of maceration that she hadn't been in the water long. As Davidson noted these initial details, Claire forced herself to stare at the girl, or woman (she corrected herself in her head). This was a woman just like her.

It wasn't the first dead body she'd seen and not the first murdered body either. However, she felt a nervous excitement when she thought how it might be the first case where she could provide some kind of justice for the woman that had floated so carelessly on the water's surface.

As Claire was staring at the corpse Gerry McKay appeared behind her. She was forced to step out of the cool, dark ambulance to allow McKay in to see the body. She stepped into the glare of the sun and the nausea hit her. Vomit scratched at the back of her throat.

'She's one of Ritchie Gordon's girls,' McKay's stark voice carried out of the vehicle and into the sunshine. Claire forced herself to gulp back down that morning's cereal as McKay stepped out of the ambulance.

'Right love, let's go and pay Ritchie a visit.'

✪

'Hardly the 'Friendly Games' if you cannae find a bit of female company in the whole city,' declared McKay three hours later as they left their fourth pub with no sign of Ritchie Gordon, or any of the prostitutes who worked for him.

Claire trotted behind McKay as they dodged tourists on the

King George Bridge. She stopped momentarily to glance back at the curve of the river and beyond to the northwest where they'd found the girl that morning.

From this vantage point the city looked stunning. The sun glinted off the armoured shoulders of the Auditorium and the rounded Hydro building, which sat like some alien craft. The shiny curve of the squinty bridge framed the whole sparkling vision. Tourists scrambled to take photos of this modern river and its skyline as if they were in NYC and Claire had to slalom through them to keep up with McKay. 'There's one more place,' he called back. 'Just didn't think he'd be in the centre of town today.'

They found Ritchie Gordon in a dingy pub under the Central Bridge. He sat on his own in a glass booth, nursing a pint, reading a paper, and emitting a 'don't even fucking try tae sit down beside me' look to tourists.

McKay eased in beside him and Ritchie looked up.

'Detective Sergeant,' he said loudly, 'Good day to you. How are ye keeping on this fine day? Should ye no be controlling proceedings at the archery, or were they worried someone would aim right at ye?'

'Know this lassie?' asked McKay bluntly. He indicated to Claire and she slid the lock on her smart phone.

She held up the photo steadily, thinking McKay was watching her. But his eyes were on Ritchie, whose bravado had sunk into the sticky carpet.

He gulped, 'Fuck me, that's Claire.' Claire gripped the phone tighter and ignored the skip of her heart. They shared a name, so what.

Ritchie's face seemed to leach colour and his eyes darted quickly round the pub. 'She was in here last night. But she doesnae work fir me anymair. There's a new guy running some aw the Polish lassies and Claire wis kinda seeing him…'

'Right so he was her boyfriend?' asked Claire, sliding into the booth beside him, lowering her voice.

'Sort aw hen. I don't know his real name. Everyone calls him Drago, know like Ivan Drago.'

'As in Rocky Four?'

✪

'I bet that's him,' said Claire stabbing at the screen as they watched the CCTV footage from the pub the night before. Their victim was standing at the bar in black trousers and a red top. The man who approached her towered over her and had bright blonde, almost white hair.

'Ivan Drago indeed,' said McKay. 'He shouldn't be hard to track down.'

Claire forwarded the tape as the pair drank at the bar. Then she paused it when they left at 8.24pm.

'Okay, we know she was with him. Let's find Drago. I'm pretty sure he'll be known to the vice boys,' said McKay. Claire knew there were two female detectives in the Vice Squad but she bit her tongue.

✪

Krystian Bakula was a Glaswegian by birth, born to Polish parents, and not as McKay had uttered, 'One of they fuckin' EU migrants.' He was known as Kris and spoke with an altogether Glaswegian accent.

'Ah've telt ye Detective Sergeant, Claire wis ma burd. Dae ye think Ah'd send ma bird oot on the streets?'

Kris covered his face with his hands and shook his head. When he finally took them away he had tears in his eyes.

'Ah canne tell yez anymair. She went tae meet some pals, Ah left her in Central.'

'So you just met your girlfriend for half an hour, then you went your separate ways? Didn't you want to spend the evening together?' asked Claire.

'Aye, but she'd made plans so Ah popped intae the pub tae

say hi, and we wur gonnae meet up the next day… Ah mean the day.'

'So ye weren't worried when she didn't contact you today?' asked McKay.

'Listen, Claire wis an addict, they're no the most reliable burds.'

✪

'You'll need to release him,' said Linda Davidson two hours later. 'His alibi checks out.'

'Ah bet it bloody does, but he's guilty,' shouted McKay.

'I'm sorry Gerry, but we need to let him go for now. I'll give you and Claire more time to work this, see what else you can turn up tomorrow,' she said, leaving Claire and McKay standing alone in the corridor.

McKay's face was bright red and he was taking deep breaths with his eyes closed. He appeared to be counting to ten.

'DS McKay, are you ok?'

'Aye hen,' answered McKay slumping over in one of the flimsy plastic seats that lined the corridor.

'Are you counting?'

'Aye…Ma therapist told me to do it when I'm raging,' he said on an out breath.

Claire bit her bottom lip and tried to stifle the giggle that was rising up at the thought of the belligerent Gerry McKay visiting his therapist. She remembered a documentary she'd seen about high-flying businessmen attending hug therapy to relieve their stress and the image of McKay in a hug of trust flitted across her mind.

She reached out her hand, as if to rub his hunched over back, but she quickly pulled it away as McKay sat up straight and looked at her.

'Don't tell anyone about the therapy. It's an anger management thing. They made me go,' he said, inclining his head towards the management offices at the end of the corridor.

—

'Sure, of course,' said Claire, nodding so vigorously it hurt her head.

✪

All the way home she thought about Claire. When she was in town with her friends ignoring the men who chatted them up at the bar, other women were waiting for any man, desperately touting themselves despite the danger they faced.

She got back to the flat and took a shower. It had been a long day but at least she'd held her own with McKay. After the shower she lay on her bed with the towel wrapped round her. Then she had an idea. She dried her hair, put on some heavy make-up and thought about a short skirt. But she decided against it and pulled on some jeans.

The Broomielaw was an area of the town that had been regenerated. If you read some council promotional material it would be described as a "commercial hub." Indeed, several large companies owned vast office space in the area. But after 6pm the Broomielaw was deserted and it had become the home of the city's prostitutes. On the outskirts of the city centre, away from the hotels and restaurants, they were left to their own devices.

Claire's heart started to beat heavily as she approached. It was 11pm and the streets were eerie compared to the Commonwealth energy of the centre. A few women stood on the corner. Some wore the stereotype knee high boots and short skirt, but others looked like mums who had just dropped their kids off at school, standing around in tracksuits tops and jeans.

She slowed the car down and switched the lights off. Her hands were clammy and the night suddenly felt oppressive. If anyone knew what she was doing she'd be disciplined. What if she did get some nugget of information, she could hardly tell McKay how she'd got it. 'Well DS McKay I just went on my own to interview the city's prostitutes and see if they knew anything about this guy who might have killed one of them.' That would definitely instigate a trip to his therapist and she could imagine his response: 'Who the fuck do ye think ye are hen? The Caped Crusader? Catwoman?'

She Claire Mitchell was an idiot. She switched the lights on again and was about to drive away when there was an abrupt rapping on the driver side window. She looked out then recoiled in horror as Gerry McKay peered in at her.

'Fuck,' muttered Claire, as McKay walked round the front of the car to the passenger side and tried the door. He rattled it up and down, but it was locked. For a moment Claire considered driving off - 'No, couldn't have been me Sarge.' Then she pressed the unlock button.

McKay got in the car. He looked at her strangely; they sat silently for a few seconds until Claire squeaked, 'Sorry Sergeant.' Her voice went higher on the last syllable so it became a question rather than a statement.

'What the fuck Claire? You shouldn't be skulking about here on your own.'

'I know. I'm sorry. It's just I couldn't stop thinking about her and she's called Claire and...'

'Ok, ok...' he held up his hand to silence her. 'Doing stupid shit like this is what I do. It gets you up in front of a disciplinary and it can even get you sent to a therapist.'

They both started to laugh. 'Listen, but now you're here, how's about talking to these lassies. They'll trust you more than me. I'll just be sitting here...so don't worry.'

Claire gulped and nodded. He glanced down at her jeans and trainers.

'Well at least you look like a Glaswegian hooker.' She smiled and got out of the car. She smiled and got out of the car. It seemed she had more in common with one of *them* than she thought. After all, both she and Gerry understood the importance of counting slowly to ten.

The Foreshot

David Warde

The Foreshot is an atmospheric historical novel set against the backdrop of the death of Queen Victoria, the Excise Acts and the second Boer War. A novel with a terrific sense of place, it takes its title from the first stage of the whisky still, the illegal distilling of which provides one of several criminal flavours to this multi-layered story of revenge, war and dramatic social upheaval.

The Foreshot is the first book of a planned trilogy.

Marcus Chatto felt the life-force flowing through him as he planned his subtle attack. There was nothing that made him feel quite as good as tearing someone else's life apart. Particularly if it was a bloody toff. For a second he allowed his mind to drift back to his Lambeth childhood, and the aristocratic bitch staring straight through him from inside her carriage. He would visualise her ice-maiden face when he shattered his victim's life and stomped on the broken pieces. With a huge effort he recalled himself to the present, and issued his instructions like a general directing his troops for battle.

'Nell, get the game set up for a week's time. Skins, you make sure that streak of piss William Less gets to hear about it. But play it cagey, understand? Don't make it too easy for him to find out about it or even a twerp like 'im'll smell a rat.' Both the hotel owner and the attack dog nodded.

'Skins, in the game, you're the stalkin' 'orse yeah?' By nodding sagely Skinner just about succeeded in hiding the fact that he had not a clue what a stalking horse was. His boss continued talking. 'Make sure all 'is attention is on you, we'll make 'im fink he's beaten yer, an' 'e won't even notice e's getting' bled white.' The nodding continued.

'Spence, same fing fer you. You'll be droppin' a bundle on the table, 'e'll pick up most of it early on.' The fifth man standing at the table also nodded, he had done this often enough.

'Jimmy, you're the ace in the hole.' Chatto chuckled at his own wit, and continued. 'We don't want 'im to even notice you're there right, so I need you lookin' old and potless. You'll lose a bit on the first few 'ands, an' yer gotta make it look like you're a right pigeon. Then when 'e finks 'e's won, you'll swoop in an' scoop it all, got it?'

The diminutive and insignificant-looking individual acquiesced with a slant of his head. Unknown in most of London, but a legend in the illegal gaming rooms, his mousy demeanour hid a brain like a steel trap. He could remember all fifty-two cards in a pack, calculate odds in the blink of an eye, and was the mathematical genius behind many of Chatto's gambling scams.

'Daisy, just make sure 'e's distracted at the right point in time yeah?' The London gangster grinned wolfishly at the striking looking girl in front of him. At the age of nineteen she had seen most of what life had to offer her, and with the aid of long practice hid her feelings of revulsion behind an imperturbable mask. She would do her job, get paid, have sex with Chatto if she had to, and focus on the money. Daisy had firm plans for a better life which she was not sharing with anyone.

Chatto received affirmative nods all round. Whilst Nellie and Daisy departed to return to the hotel, the five men broke open half a dozen new packs of cards. Under the direction of Jimmy *the brains* Lenthall, Chatto's tame sharp, they laid them out on the table, then re-gathered each pack in a specific order. They dealt three practice hands to ensure that the sequence was correct, then re-sealed the packs with cowgum in the original brown paper packaging.

✪

The large bundles of bank notes in William Less's pockets were a comforting presence. Simply holding the cash on his person restored his self-esteem, and he could already feel the tingle of anticipation in his stomach. His interview with Isaac Stewart at the Royal Bank of Scotland had not improved his humour. The man had clearly forgotten rightful place in life, which was to serve his betters. He was remarkably reluctant to release money from the Glensgurr account, but faced with the fact that William was one of the co-signatories, he had had little alternative and gave in with bad grace. William rode away fuming, his chagrin only mollified by satisfaction at having found a meaningful game. In a couple of days he would be away from heather, whisky and shitty weather, back where he belonged in the fleshpots of London.

The venue for the game was the back room of a hotel in Lambeth, just south of the river. Anyone wishing to enter the gaming room had to pass through two separate locked doors, each guarded by a thug with a cudgel, and submit to a body search on the way. Once inside the room, the only constant sounds were the dry rustle of cards as they were played, and the subdued clink of glasses being re-filled. The gently hissing gas-light spilled brightness over the green baize table and threw dancing shadows into the nether spaces. The game was hosted by Nelly Sempill, the hard-faced owner of the hotel. Avaricious to a fault, she had inherited the business when her husband died, and the local rumour was that she had rendered his body down for soap in order to make a quick profit.

Games in her hotel were played by her rules, no questions and no exceptions. She explained those rules in a grating south London accent.

'Right gentlemen, this is how it is. We're playing poker, twenty guineas buys you in, minimum stake two guineas on any hand. I'm the dealer, and that doesn't change. Any tricks you think you know I probably invented, so we'll have no funny business. If I say you're out you're out, and if you don't like it you can take it up with the boys outside. If you don't like what someone else is doing you object through me. There's no metal on the table at any time, Daisy'll get you drinks and ashtrays when you need them.'

She didn't even bother asking if there were any questions, it wasn't that sort of game.

William Less took stock of his fellow players. A man called Skinner, scar-faced and leering was opposite, malevolence seeping out of his every pore. A huge bulldog lay at his feet, following his every move with cold black eyes. A florid and flashily-dressed individual by the name of Spencer Brummel was to his right, and to his left was possibly the most unremarkable man he had ever seen. Introduced as James Lenthall, Will would have taken him for a bank clerk. His suit was shiny with age, the collar frayed, and the shoes down at heel. His fingernails were bitten down to the quick, and dandruff constantly dropped from his head onto the dark green baize. The fingers of his left hand were stained brown with nicotine, indicating a heavy smoking habit. But he had paid his way in, and gambling tended to attract an odd crowd.

Less was looking forward to humiliating the other players with his refined system at cards, and reducing his debt at the same time.

Nellie removed the stiff paper wrapper from a pack of cards and dropped it on the floor. Quickly and efficiently she removed the jokers and the score card from the pack and started to shuffle. Her movements were slick and practised, the pasteboards riffling quietly as she separated, sifted and merged them all back into a neat block.

She placed the pack between her and Skinner, one place to her left, and he cut them. Nellie picked up the bottom half, placed them on top and began the deal. Five cards landed in front of each player and were picked up, inspected, and re-ordered. There was no chat, nor any need for it, this was a professionals' game.

Whilst seeming to focus entirely on the hands that had been dealt, each player was surreptitiously monitoring the others, looking for the tells. Only the very best players truly have a poker face. Many amateurs think they do, or like to think so, but an experienced sharp will notice even the subliminal signs. Rapid blinking, accelerated breathing, or a longer draw on a cigar are all obvious to a practised gambler.

William was especially careful to give nothing away, but an average hand of two of clubs, seven of hearts, jack of diamonds, nine of spades and ace of clubs was not that much to get excited about anyway. It was a good warm-up hand, and he mentally settled into what would be a long night.

The waitress's silk skirt briefly brushed his shoulder as she walked behind him. The contact was so minimal that it must have been accidental, although watching her from the corner of his eye, he noticed that she did not come that close to any other player. He suspected she fancied him, and his feeling of well-being increased. Common girls often went for him, it was the lethal combination of good looks, plentiful money and easy charm.

William reminded himself sternly that he didn't have any money at the moment, and felt a pang of guilt when he remembered that he was gambling with his sister's earnings. He re-focussed on his cards. With his seven, nine, jack and ace he could aim for a straight. The ace and two of clubs were not much good to him; aces were high, although he was thinking of the basis of a flush.

Skinner, sitting on Nellie's left was the first to bet, and he staked two guineas, a sensible minimum. Everyone matched the stake or raised it around the table. The scruffy looking Lenthall was already smoking, holding a cheroot in his left hand and cards in his right. As the cards lay face up on the table, William ended up with three jacks, one in his hand and two in the middle. But he was trumped by a flush from the ostentatious Spencer Brummel on his right.

That was fine, it was better to lose the small hands early in the game, whilst everyone was settling into a rhythm. And he had the entire Glensgurr bank balance converted into chips in front of him, so he could afford to lose now and again.

Five hundred miles to the north Tom and Nicola were at Cateran's Dub, supposedly helping out with a distilling run. Actually they were lying under a blanket some distance from the still, exploring each other's bodies. She had asked him to kiss her in the most intimate places, and he had been immensely aroused by her frankness. It was a strange sensation for him to be using his tongue between her legs, and the taste of her was nothing like he had imagined. But he enjoyed it, and to judge from her reaction, so did she.

Nicola felt *liberated*. With her business ventures going well, the estate debt being reduced, and the real prospect of local youngsters staying in Glensgurr, she felt on top of the world. Contrary to everything she had been brought up to believe, she was living proof that women could succeed in business. She had the heady feeling of changing the world, breaking free from the stifling shackles of a strait-laced childhood. She only wished that her father was still around to witness her success. And as a bonus, she was enjoying inventive, if infrequent, sex with the man she loved. Sensitive to feelings in the village, she judged the time not yet right for the two of them to declare their relationship publicly, so she insisted on discretion. It curtailed their opportunities, but increased their passion when they did meet. Nights at the Dub were not to be missed.

At around midnight, William's hand of cards in Lambeth was the thing that gamblers dream of. He was dealt *two* aces in his hand of five. Straight away he could beat any other pair. But better was to follow. He also had an eight, and when those on the table were turned up, glory be, there was a second eight, a queen and a third ace. Full house, aces and eights. A child could have told you that he was on a winning hand.

Statistically, the chances of anyone beating that were virtually nil, so he piled into the betting. He pushed two five-guinea chips into the centre of the baize, the ivory counters clicking softly as they came to rest. The room froze, transfixed by the size of the stake, and even Daisy paused in her movements. Lenthall recovered first, throwing his cards face-down onto the table. He was out. He took a long drag from his cigar with his left hand, and made a great pretence of studying the glowing tip. The smoke rose slowly to join the dense cloud already clinging to the stained ceiling.

Spencer Brummel swore loudly, and threw his hand down with ill-concealed chagrin, thereby sacrificing his chips as well. That left only the scar-faced tough. As they locked eyes, the challenge silently issued and accepted, William remembered that his name was Skinner. He lifted a sardonic eyebrow, daring the man to stay with him. Skinner raised him a further five guineas, then scratched an angry-looking sore underneath his stubble. Was that a tell? William matched him for the last time, still with a faint smile. Skinner laid out his cards, including the two black queens. With the queen of hearts already in the middle of the table that gave him three of a kind, court cards. It was a tough hand to beat, but William's full house flattened it.

As he scooped up forty five guineas, William smiled broadly. He knew it was a breach of etiquette to celebrate good hands in a professional game, but he simply could not stop himself grinning with delight. Forty-five guineas in one hand! This was how a man should live! The little people might be content weaving tartan and breeding cows, but making forty-five guineas at one hand of poker placed him way above the little people. Staring mesmerised at his growing stack of chips, he missed Daisy's glance, a strange mix of scorn and pity.

He had also missed the intense and steady scrutiny from the unremarkable James Lenthall to his left. The sharp was not only a great card player, but also an astute judge of character. Everything that happened in the game was at his behest, deliberately set up so that he could judge the character of the man he was fleecing.

Brummel's swearing, Skinner's betrayal of nerves, Daisy's subtle flirting and the winning hands were all set up so that he could peer into Less's soul. If he saw even one thing he wasn't sure of, he would call off the game there and then. But he knew he now had the measure of the young aristocrat in front of him; vain, excitable and rich. A card sharp's dream. He was ready to move in for the kill.

Pigeon-holes

Sarah Palmer

When my mother says your brother-in-law I can't think who she's talking about. She likes her pigeon-holes, my mother, and I have to say that over the years they've proved themselves to be handy storage. Every so often, during one of her extended visits up from the coast, she'll dust off a pigeon-hole and there'll be a story about my aunt, your father's cousin, your grandmother. We can spend a comfortable morning, or at least an hour, as I nod along to a familiar story, punctuated here and there with something she's heard from other people, maybe my friend's sister or your uncle's dentist. But the cast of characters is pretty steadfast, reliable. As you'd expect from a woman of her age and temperament.

So when she's wiping toast crumbs from the corner of her mouth and says your brother-in-law, I search my memory for someone else. A person who has performed some kind of transgression by making a misjudged remark in time of sorrow perhaps, or arrived at a family gathering with a thoughtless cheesecake.

She taps at the Daily Mail splayed in front of her on the kitchen table, and points at a blurred photograph, beckoning me over with her toast. I don't want to look at the Daily Mail, I don't even want it in the house if I'm honest, but some arguments just aren't worth having. My father's cousin was a Conservative councillor and he…

Her mouth's full of toast again so my mother's now tapping the paper with some force. I sigh and peer over her shoulder at the CCTV still. I'd misunderstood. My mother hadn't said your brother-in-law, like she was starting a story. No, it was a question - your brother-in-law?

Sitting down next to her I pull the newspaper towards me. She's right, it is him, with his new name and new beard and seeming new-found ability to get out of bed before three o'clock in the afternoon. I would have turned the page without recognising him, since we stopped looking for him a long time ago. But somehow my mother clocked him - even though she only met him once, in a wedding line-up when he was clean-shaven, happy to be called Stevo and charm the birds from the trees.

Later, when Mike's come back from work and rung the police, and his dad, and his other brother, and cried, my mother makes ham and cheese sandwiches and goes to have a nap.

Perhaps, if she hadn't been visiting at just the right time, she wouldn't have remembered him either, just glanced at the photograph like the rest of us and put him in some other pigeon-hole. Not had to sneak off to her bedroom with her mobile for a whispered conversation, my daughter's brother-in-law…

The Phoenix

Nichola Deadman

'What's that?' said Maggie sharply, her knitting falling into her lap.

'What's what, love?'

'Can you not smell that? Something's burning.'

Gerald tilted his head and sniffed. He opened his mouth to tell her she was imagining things but then the scent came to him also. He stood up quickly. 'Did you turn the gas off?'

'Yes of course.' Maggie stood up too now. 'You have a look in the yard and I'll check the house.'

'Aye, alright.'

Gerald did not need to check the yard: when he opened the back door the smell was much stronger. For a stupid moment he thought the dawn had come, then the image resolved itself into a dancing orange line that ran the entire length of his barley field.

'Maggie!' he shouted, feeling the panic rear inside him and trying to quell it, to stay calm enough to do the thousand things that needed doing now. '*Maggie!*'

'What's... *oh!*'

Gerald opened his mouth to tell her to phone the police, the fire brigade, the neighbours, but the words died on his lips.

There was something moving, out in front of the flames. Or were his eyes playing tricks on him? It was hard to see from this distance, but in the firelight he thought he could discern a person moving.

No... *dancing*? A wild weird caper full of savage glee. Gerald blinked. It seemed almost as though the person was on fire.

His wife stepped forward, past him, and stood staring, open-mouthed.

79

'Maggie! We need to call the fire brigade!'

But she wasn't listening. Her eyes were locked on the distant dancer. He noticed she was shaking.

'Maggie!' said Gerald again.

When she turned to him he could see the blaze reflected in her eyes. She looked terrified, more afraid than he'd ever seen her. More afraid than he'd ever seen anyone.

'Jen? Jenny love, sorry to wake you, only it's work.'

Jen Ridley groaned and sat bolt upright. 'Oh no, *please* don't tell me I'm late on the first bloody day!'

'It's six in the morning love. They called the house phone because you weren't answering your mobile.'

'Oh *shit*.' She leaned over and rattled the mobile phone on the nightstand – dead. 'I had it on charge all night!'

'Language, love. Negative words are toxic. That socket can be a bit wonky sometimes – I'll ask Rod to have a look at it this afternoon.'

Jen swung her legs out of the single bed and stood up, forcing her mind into the straightjacket of calmness. 'You said it was work?

'Oh yes, they said to tell you they're very sorry but could you please go round to the Baines farm at once? It's urgent, they said.'

No time for a shower then. Jen frowned at the pale light creeping in under the curtain. 'Thanks Mum,' she said, and reached into her suitcase for a pair of slacks and a parka. 'Sorry they woke you and Rod.'

'Oh Rod's out for his run already, he and I get up early these days.'

There was a slightly awkward silence. How would *she* know the rhythms of this household? 'Right,' she said aloud. 'Baines farm, how do I get there?'

Her mother explained as they went downstairs. 'Be careful, love,' she said, drawing her purple gown around her as Jen opened the front door.

'Thanks Mum.'

At least the Honda only took two tries to start.

Not the best kick-off to the New Life. But then when you were sleeping on a too-soft single bed in your remarried mother's guest room, what could you expect? At least she hadn't had to face Rod this morning. After dinner last night he'd fixed her with an intense look. 'We're going to help your mother through this *together*,' he'd said, and for a horrifying moment Jen had thought he would reach out and pat her arm or something.

When she'd arrived she'd half expected to see the diagnosis written on her mother's face. Not this neat little cottage with its simple, clean decorations and kitchen cupboards full of quinoa and chia seeds. Mandalas on the walls and lots of books about spirituality. It seemed to have come along with Rod, who was a slim, dapper little man with piercing eyes. Her mum was happy enough. 'He's so good to me love,' her mother had confided. 'He lost a sister when he was young, and he's determined to… well, help me through, you know. He's very spiritual.'

It was unsettling.

Not as unsettling, however, as the man ahead, who was standing in the middle of the road and waving her to a halt. Behind him she could see sheep emerging from a hedgerow and trotting across the road. It started as a trickle.

After a few minutes Jen rolled down the window. 'Excuse me! Just wondering how long this is going to take. Only I'm on police business and in a bit of a hurry.'

The man stared at her blankly.

'Do you reckon it'll be another minute or two then?'

He nodded concession to the possibility and shrugged, then turned his back on her and watched the endless ovine stream pouring across the street.

Jen rolled her eyes. New Life, she told herself. *New Life!* You're here for your Mum. And because you were bored and lonely in London. And because you were sick of it all – all the human ugliness that you saw every day on the headlong sprint to become *Detective Inspector* Jen Ridley. Depressed Idiot, more like.

Christ, can't I just have a single sheep-interrupted drive without an existential crisis?

It was then that she noticed the distant wisps of smoke.

The Baines farmyard was chaotic with fire engines, police cars and a group of exhausted-looking and soot-stained men. She could see the blackened field beyond the trampled rows of barley; bits of it were still smoking. Jen parked and walked towards the densest concentration of people. She caught sight of a uniform.

'Excuse me, officer,' she called out. Twelve years on the job had perfected the voice of authority: he looked round at once. 'I'm DI Jen Ridley…'

'How nice of you to join us, DI Ridley.' It came from behind her so that she was the one who had to turn. 'Walk with me please.'

A tall figure strode by. She had a fleeting impression of salt-and-pepper hair and a beaky nose, and she scrambled to follow, biting down excuses.

'DCI John Ross,' he barked over his shoulder. 'On my way to interview the farm owners now, Gerald and Maggie Baines.'

'Er… arson Sir?'

'Certainly looks that way. We share a fire specialist with the rest of the district and he should be here later today, but I think we can work on that premise, all things given.' He did not elaborate, but paused at the farm door, dug in a pocket and handed her a badge on a lanyard. 'Best put that on.'

The farm kitchen was as busy as the yard outside. A youngish man was running water over his reddened hands and a couple of middle-aged women were doing things with platters and cellophane. "Better get those sandwiches out to the lads," one was saying. 'They've had a hard night.'

'Hullo Sylvia,' said DCI Ross. 'Where are Gerald and

—

82

Maggie?'

'Sitting room.' The woman shook her head. 'They're taking it hard. Sandwich?'

'No thanks.'

Jen, who hadn't eaten since the previous day, watched the sandwiches head out of the kitchen door with regret.

Gerald and Maggie Baines were huddled on a couch, holding each other's hands and talking in low voices. They fell silent when DCI Ross opened the door, but Jen caught the words, '…go to your sister's… not safe…'

Maggie looked from Ross's face to Jen's. 'You'll not catch him,' she said, her voice hard. 'There's nothing for it but for us to leave.'

'Maggie…' said Gerald, and stopped, looking unsure.

'I assure you we'll do our best to find the perpetrator,' said DCI Ross.

'… *Him*?' said Jen.

Maggie regarded her for a moment, as though sizing her up. 'Aye. We saw Him last night.'

'You mean you saw who lit the fires?'

'I mean we saw the Him dancing by the flames. I'm *telling* you… he's back.'

Jen opened her mouth to ask a question but they were interrupted by a knock on the door and a young constable stuck his head in the room. "Excuse me, Sir," he said, addressing DCI Ross, 'but there's something I think you'll want to see.'

Ross told Jen the story as they followed the constable across the burned out field. She was glad of the distraction from what the sooty, stubbly, charred plant stalks were doing to her brand new trainers, and made a mental note to invest in a pair of Wellies as soon as humanly possible.

'It's a bit… weird,' Ross said, shaking his head. 'Silly almost, if it weren't so bad.'

83

Nearly two decades before, a series of fires had gone through the area. At first the targets were crops near harvest, which was devastating to the local farmers. Two or three farmers were ruined and had to sell up and move elsewhere. The police questioned everyone from the local kids to passing travellers. They searched for insurance scams. Nobody really seemed to fit the bill.

But after that the targets got more threatening. A storage shed set alight one evening while no one was home. A garage fire at two o'clock in the morning, narrowly prevented from setting the house ablaze with the family asleep inside. Those families packed up and left too, fearing a house fire would be next.

So when another field was set alight people were almost relieved.

Until they found the body.

Someone had been bound with nylon cord and left in the middle of the field to die. It was a local woman, about twenty years old.

And then the fires stopped. Just like that. Never another.

'Those were the facts,' Ross said. 'The strange part was that every time there was a fire, people claimed to see someone – a man, they thought – dancing near the flames. He was never caught or recorded so some people thought he might not be…' Ross paused and frowned, '*real.*'

'That's ridiculous,' said Jen before she could stop herself.

'I'm inclined to agree. You saw Maggie though. Her family was one of the few that stayed behind. She's not the type to scare easily, but…'

'Here it is,' said the constable.

Spray painted across the black stubble in white letters were the words

FIRE BRINGS NEW LIFE

New Life… Jen shivered.

By the time Jen got home that night she was utterly exhausted. She'd spent the rest of the day at the station, having a "proper introduction" to her new colleagues and reviewing case files. At least she'd had a chance to charge her phone at a working socket.

As she pulled the Honda into the yard a slim figure moved through her headlights – Rod, she supposed, and grimaced at the thought of facing him. He seemed to be loading something bulky into the boot of his own car but when he saw her he turned and stared for a moment.

He stormed up to her car even before she'd come to a complete stop, and slapped a hand down on the car's bonnet. The sound was shockingly loud.

'Where the *hell* have you been? Your mother was worried sick!' He was shouting and there was an edge in his voice. 'You're disrupting everything by coming in at this hour! She needs rest! She's sick!'

Jen wondered if she'd get in trouble for arresting her mother's husband. She wasn't frightened so much as disturbed – Rod had always been mild-mannered enough around her, and her mother certainly would never have put up with verbal abuse.

She opened the car door. 'Rod,' she said, feeling strange for using the Police Voice on someone she knew. 'Don't talk to me like…'

He was *so quick*. Like a boxer. The blow came from nowhere, something long and heavy he'd been concealing in the darkness.

The last thing Jen saw as she tumbled to the ground was a bit of purple terrycloth hanging out of his car's boot.

No, she thought, when she came to. No, no, no. Please no. *Mum!*

Her head was screaming with pain as she pushed herself off the ground and scrabbled inside the car for her mobile. Three missed calls from DCI Ross. *NO!*

She was fumbling with her phone when it started ringing again.

'DI Ridley, you really need to start making yourself available…'

'My mum…'

'What?'

'He's got my mum!' She forced herself to calm down. 'I think… my mum's husband, I think he's kidnapped my mum. He hit me with something heavy – he knocked me out but I think…' Jen shut her eyes against the throbbing in her head. 'I think he's going to set another field on fire tonight and… he's got my *mum*!' She swallowed the sob.

'Stay where you are,' said Ross, 'I'll get someone to you as soon as I can.'

Jen persisted. His car! Get people looking for his car!'

There was a short silence on the other end of the line. 'Just stay where you are alright? No matter what.'

But Jen had seen the distant orange glow on the horizon. He'd lit fires already.

She felt the air leave her lungs.

Hours later, at the station. Jen watched the questioning room on the monitor, feeling sick and detached.

'I gave them new lives, don't you see? I gave them the beautiful cataclysm that forced them into change. Fire is a cleansing agent. I've always known that, ever since I was a child!' Rod thumped his chest.

DCI Ross stared at him from across the table. They were down the hall, and the little black and white screen leached away the malice she'd felt from him before. He just looked very, very convinced. Very earnest.

It was the most frightening thing she'd ever seen.

'We left after my sister… she was so ill, *so* ill! Leukemia! She was only nineteen. And the only way to help her live was to just wipe the slate clean, you know? Purify everything. So she could live again, reborn from the ashes. A new life!'

—

86

Jen started at the knock on the door behind her, and stood up. 'Mum!'

'We've just finished with her,' said a young paramedic, who was holding her mum's arm. 'A bit out of it, but alright.'

'Oh Jen!" Her mum stepped forward and they held each other for a long time. "Oh *Jen!* If you hadn't come… I had no idea he was…'

'It's alright, Mum.' Even though it wasn't. 'We'll figure it out, step-by-step. Move out of that cottage for one thing.'

'I want everything gone,' said her mother fiercely. 'New everything. A new life.'

Jen stared at the monitor, where Rod had gone silent.

The Letter

Kerrie McKinnel

Violet glanced around the office.

'Hello?'

No answer. She headed for the desk. 'Sarah dear, if you want the cash to be secure then you should change the pin once in a while,' Violet muttered to herself. Her fingers skipped across the worn keypad. Two hundred? Too much. Someone would notice. She tucked half into her pocket. New shoes perhaps, or a meal out.

The office was stuffy and smelt of Sarah's tuna sandwich. Violet glanced at the clock. There was time for a walk to the newsagents. 'Ahem.' Violet spun around and bumped against the desk.

'Sarah. You're back early. Good meeting?' Sarah closed the door. The sun glinted off the frosted glass panel.

'You promised you'd stop.'

'I didn't do anything, I ...'

'Please Vi, stop lying. I can't keep covering for you.'

'Oh, stop acting the saint. I never asked you to do anything except leave me alone.' Violet pushed past to get to the door.

'Vi, wait.' Sarah took a letter out of her handbag.

'What's that?'

'My resignation.'

'What?' Violet stared at the envelope, addressed to Mr Reed.

'I'm confessing to your thefts. All you need to do is stop, and you can forget it ever happened.'

'But what if he sues you, or ... You didn't do anything.'

Sarah took Violet's hands and squeezed. 'Mum would kill me if I let anything happen to my little sister. Anyway, don't worry about me. He's still very sympathetic since finding out Lynne has disabilities.' She sighed. 'I suppose I'll have to put that trip to Disneyland on hold, but I wasn't sure it was such a good idea anyway. It'd be so hard for her, watching all the other kids from her wheelchair. No. Really. We'll be fine.'

'But Mr Reed hasn't even noticed the money's missing.'

'He asked me about it last week,' said Sarah. 'And it won't be long until he asks again. Honestly Vi, it's for the best.'

'No, I ...

The office door opened. 'Afternoon ladies,' said Mr Reed.

'Could I have a quick word?' asked Sarah.

He checked his watch. 'I've got a few minutes before my next meeting. Come on in.'

Violet watched her big sister walk towards their boss's office.

And then, she heard the words escaping out of her own mouth.

'It was me.'

'Sorry?' said Mr Reed, turning around.

'I took the money. I've been stealing for months.' It spilled out like the blood when Violet was seven and she fell off her bike doing wheelies. Sarah took the blame then too. 'It was me,' Violet repeated.

'I see,' said Mr Reed. His brows furrowed. 'Violet, could I see you in my office? Now.'

Sarah waited for the door to close behind them, and then, with a relieved smile, she ripped the empty envelope in two and dropped it into the bin. There was half an hour left of lunchtime. Still time to pop to the travel agents.

Hannah

Katy Simmonds

The window of the girls' changing rooms never gets shut. Maybe they don't think that anyone would dare to break in, or maybe they think it's too small to fit through. But that window is my only chance. Did they think I'd be afraid to skip meals when something as important as revenge is at stake?

No one should steal. Hannah knows that; she's meant to be my friend. I forgave her when she started wearing her hair like mine – actually I was flattered, but then she starts showing up at my house uninvited, acting all sweet and polite in front of my parents. Suddenly she's always with my friends, who absolutely love This New Hannah. She kissed Adam Flynn. She knew I liked him, but she did it anyway.

And no one realises what she's doing because she's so...nice. And she's always crying. That's how she gets people to like her. And nothing I say makes any difference; people just leap to her defence. When I see her crying, I want to slap her.

Mum and Dad say that if I keep hitting people I'll eventually wind up alone, but they have no idea what this is like. Real friends don't steal from each other – simple as that. Hannah broke the rules, so now I'm going to do something about it.

The window seems smaller than I remember; up close the frame is rusty and littered with the bodies of dead flies that disintegrate at my touch. I recoil, wiping my hands on my jeans. It wasn't this small in my head, wasn't this filthy, this real.

You're being pathetic. Stop it.

I'm shivering, but I take off my jumper and throw it inside, before putting my arms through, trying to ignore the flies. I take a deep breath and put my head through carefully, but I still manage to snag my hairband on the frame. A few strands of hair come loose and trail through the fly-mess beneath me.

Oh God...this is horrible. Grow up.

Holding my breath, I force each shoulder a little further forwards, in turn. The skin on my arms goes red and sore looking, but it's working. Eventually, I give one final push and my shoulders are through.

Now for the rest of me, but I'm exhausted; sweating and panicking. I can't move. I'm stuck. What am I going to do? I'll just have to wait until I'm discovered. But how will I explain myself? I'm pretty used to getting into trouble for fighting, but breaking into school is a whole new level.

I start wriggling, ignoring how much it hurts. I imagine those dead flies coming back to life and crawling over me; I see Hannah, surrounded by all my friends and family and I hear an angry thudding sound in my ears. I push hard against the inner wall, straining and twisting.

Then I'm sliding through and landing on the back of my neck with my legs and body on top, making my stomach contract uncomfortably like someone's been using me as an accordion. I made it though. Nothing else matters.

✪

This place looks so different at night; there's nothing to distract you from the stains in the plastic ceiling tiles, or the scratches kids made along the walls with their keys. I walk past my locker, still dented from the time I slammed Danny Tan into it after he spat in my hair.

Danny never got punished, but I did. Suddenly I had a Bad Attitude; suddenly I had to talk about it to strangers, had to discuss my issues in special groups for people with my type of Problematic Behaviour.

I ought to be nice, they told me, not aggressive, not violent. Well I tried being nice – I really did. But I'm not nice. That's not who I am.

And then there was Hannah, suddenly next to me in Maths. And it wasn't just Maths; it was every lesson. We'd been put together for everything, like peas in a pod, apparently.

I'd never seen her before and she was obviously new 'cos no one else had heard of her. I felt kind of sorry for her; her good behaviour had got her sat next to the mean girl on her first day.

Nice, sweet Hannah, who stole my friends. Gentle Hannah, who knew everything about me, yet said so little of herself. Never even told me her surname. After tonight though, there'll be no Hannah.

Even in the dark, I know my way to the Headmistress' office. And right next to that – Student Records. No more hiding Hannah, I'm going to find you.

✪

I don't believe it. I've gone through the whole of Year 8 and she's not here. There should be four Hannahs, including her, but I can only find three. I've even looked in the other years, but nothing. No Hannah. Where is she?

I pick up the two other Hannahs' files again, examining them carefully, pressing my nose right up to the portrait of each girl, but it's neither of them. I fling Hannah Matthews' file across the room; it flaps uselessly, belching out detention slips and sick notes over the Secretary's desk.

There are files everywhere. There's no way I can put these back the way they were. I should go home. I should just go home right now. I muddle up the files on the floor, stuffing the Hannahs to the bottom, then shuffling it all again, just to be sure.

At the door, I look back at the mess I've made. Why isn't

Hannah's file there? Does anyone know? Maybe I should tell someone.

My watch beeps, making my whole body lurch nervously. I slap my hand over it to stifle the sound of the alarm, even though no one's around to hear. I have half an hour to get home.

✪

'But she's not a real student!' I yell. 'Okay I lied. I'm sorry…but have you heard anything I've said? She could be anyone!'

I can't believe Kim told on me. I can't believe Mum and Dad couldn't wait for me to be more than ten minutes late before freaking out and ringing Kim's house.

'This. Has. To. Stop,' Dad cries banging his fist on the dinner table in time with each word. 'Whatever this obsession is, it has to stop. Right now.'

'Obsession?' Now I'm really mad. As if I'm obsessed with Hannah? They're the ones who keep asking me the same questions over and over.

Where's Nice Hannah? Why don't we see Nice Hannah anymore?

They don't even care that she's not a real student. I'm not obsessed; I just want my life back.

'Sweetheart,' Mum chimes in, right on time. 'We're worried about you…this isn't normal.'

Normal. That's what it all boils down to; normality. They don't want a daughter who gets into fights; they want a daughter like Hannah. *Nice Hannah*, who keeps taking everyone away from me. And she'll keep on taking and taking and now I'll never stop her.

'I'm going to bed.' I say. I turn around and stomp upstairs without giving them time to respond. What's the point in fighting? Hannah's won. She can have them.

'I'm not finished with you!' yells Dad, then Mum says something I can't hear.

93

No one follows me upstairs.

Inside my room, I slam my door and turn around, ready to throw something. And she's there. She's there, stood in front of my open wardrobe with this weird look on her face.

'Were you stealing my clothes?" Why can't I think of anything better to say?

She doesn't say anything; just stands there, panting, like she's been running.

'How did you get in here?'

Again, nothing.

'Answer me!'

I hear Mum yelling downstairs, but I'm not really listening. This girl is in my room. Here's me trying to find out where she lives and she's in my room.

And then I'm right in front of her; I'm right in her face, wondering how I managed to move so fast. I knock her back into the wardrobe with a smack to the jaw. I hit her again. Punching someone really hurts and I must have knocked a tooth or something because there's blood everywhere. I keep hitting her and hitting her and she's crying out in pain now and so am I, but I don't stop hitting, because this is my chance isn't it? This is my chance to be rid of her for good.

We fall to the floor and I try to wipe my face with the back of my hand, but there's this great big shard of glass sticking out of it. How did that get there?

'Oh Han!'

Mum's at the door. Then she's beside me, pulling me away from…she's gone.

'She was in my room,' I say while Mum picks up my hands and inspects them one by one.

'What have you done?' She keeps saying it over and over

again, hugging me while Dad paces back and forth with his phone glued to his ear.

I stare at my bloody knuckles. They're starting to burn; I can feel the pieces of glass like they're pushing my bones apart, but I won't cry. I won't.

Did she go out the window? Is that where the glass came from? But the window isn't broken. There's glass in front of my wardrobe and I feel like I should know where it came from, but I don't. And my wardrobe looks different somehow. Something's missing.

'Ambulance is on its way Hannah,' Dad says, stroking my hair gently.

Scrubland

Reece McCormack

Every Tuesday morning Kiran drives to the nearest town in her pick-up. She buys us food, shit roll, magazines, sometimes a book or whatever, and a copy of all the newspapers. While she does this I go for a run. I never used to run before I came here, but now I run every day. I'm getting quite good at it. I head out between the clusters of trailers, strung together with fairy lights and reeking of moon-shine, past the toilets and the showers, and into the open scrubland. Today, when I get back, the food has been put away and the latest issues of Billboard and Rolling Stone are waiting for me on the kitchen side, along with the tampons I asked for. Andy is laid on the bed with the newspapers open and littered around him. 'We get a mention in the Chicago Tribune,' he says, not looking at me.

It's night and James, Nick and Donald are outside playing poker at the table, situated in the middle of the trailers, which are arranged in a rough circle.

'Where's Andy?' I ask as I come up to them.

'Haven't seen him,' James says, scratching at the rash of black stubble around his jaw. He pulls out one of the plastic chairs for me to sit on. 'You in?'

'Not tonight.'

Donald drops his cigarette butt in an empty beer can. 'I saw him earlier with Kiran. They're doing that,' he cuts through the air with a karate chop. 'Kung Fu, Jujitsu shit. Whatcha call it?'

When I find Andy, Kiran is slamming him into the dirt. The lumberjack shirt she usually wears is draped over a dying shrub behind her trailer and she's stripped down to her vest. Her straggly hair is tied up in a bun. Andy rolls to the left and jumps to his feet, his side black with mud, and lunges at Kiran. She sidesteps him, takes his arm, does some crazy trick, and Andy goes down, face-first in the dirt, Kiran's knee in his spine.

The scene is lit up by a strand of fairy lights, blinking green and blue and red, twisted around the side of Kiran's trailer. She gets off, lets Andy up, and the two of them go at it again. I stand there and watch them fight, waiting for one of them to notice me.

This isn't going to be like last time. That's what Andy says, back at our trailer. We're on the bed and he leans forward and kisses me and tells me it's a promise. 'We're engaged now.' He takes my hand in his, which is dirty, grazed and bleeding, and waves it in my face. 'You see that ring?'

'Fuck off, Andy.' I pull my hand back. 'Don't patronise me like that.'

I get off the bed and grab a Coke from the mini fridge. Andy sits on the duvet and rattles out the same old about him and Kiran being friends and that he's known her since he was in college and that I know all this. I ask him why he's telling me, if I know it already.

'What do you want me to say, Chantelle? She's helping us out. She's helping us out big time.'

He waits for me to say something. The bedside lamp is on and in this light he looks ginger, like he used to. A mosquito is buzzing, fighting to get through the screen mesh protecting the window. I can hear James playing his guitar outside.

'And,' I say, pulling the tab off the Coke, 'you've fucked her before.'

'Kiran is helping us out. You're being unreasonable.' Andy shakes his head. 'She's putting herself on the line for us.'

'No, Andy.' I take a swig from the can. 'She's putting herself on the line for you.'

He tells me that's not true and I tell him that it is and that he can go fuck himself and then I go for a run.

I tire myself out and stop for a rest beside one of the dilapidated trailers. Its roof has sunken in and the windows are opaque with dust and the whole thing is tangled up in blinking coloured lights. I sit on the ground and watch my flashing silhouette. It blinks in, disappears, reappears, blinks out, reappears again. I watch this for a few minutes, then get up and tear the lights off the front of the trailer and throw them down the side. I don't know why they dress these ugly boxes up in pretty colours. The more I think about it, the less it makes sense, and I start kicking at the knot of lights and stamping on the bulbs.

I tire myself out and drop back onto the dirt.

I wish we could go back to how it used to be, before Andy freaked and shot the kid. It was just the two of us, holding up shops. It was nothing big – just corner shops and liquor stores and takeaways – but we were happy. We never took too much and we never killed anyone. The gun was just for show. I want desperately to go back to that.

Andy pins all the news clippings to the bedroom wall. The newspaper this morning described the kid as a virtuoso pianist. Andy likes to pretend that stuff doesn't get to him, but I saw the way his hand trembled as he pushed the pin through the plywood. I hear him sometimes, when he thinks I'm sleeping, whispering to himself, telling the kid he's sorry, and I pretend not to hear it, like I pretend he's not losing his hair and like I pretend that when we leave the scrubland and when we leave Kiran, it'll all go back to how it used to be.

It's Friday night and Kiran is sitting next to Andy, running her finger up and down her beer. I'm sitting between Nick on one side and James on the other. We're playing poker. Some woman – Betsy I think she's called – is sitting in the doorway of her trailer, watching us, drinking from a bottle of Heineken. She's in her underwear, her big breasts bursting from her bra and her flabby gut sagging over her panties.

'Look at them tits,' James says, staring at her over Andy's shoulder. 'Like water balloons.'

Kiran shakes her head. 'I'm out. I fold.'

'Sink your teeth into them devils.' James runs his tongue over his teeth. 'And pop.'

He takes a drink of his home-made corn whiskey. After draining the tumbler, he unscrews the decanter and pours himself another. He goes to fill my glass and I tell him that I'm okay and don't want a drink.

'No? Chantelle, what gives? You're like a drink of water.' He screws the ball back into the top of the decanter.

'I'm like what?'

'It means you're boring,' Kiran says, looking over at Andy's hand.

'I just don't feel like drinking.'

'Yeah,' Andy says. 'You feel boring.'

Later, in bed, Andy whispers into my ear, asking me what's wrong. I tell him that I'm tired and that I'm sick of this place and that I want to leave and he tells me that we just have to wait.

'We just got to hang in for a while,' he says. There's something in his voice when he says it and I lay there for a long time afterwards, staring at the paper clippings above the headrest, before I realise I don't believe him.

Sometimes I feel like crying, and sometimes, when I see Kiran, when she's alone with Andy or when they're practising Krav Maga, I want to hurt her. I see the way they look at each other, or how they drink from the same glass or share a cigarette, and I imagine all the things I could do to her.

At other times. I think about Andy and Kiran, backpacking across Europe eleven years before the two of us even met. I think about them in Italy and Greece and Germany and I think about them getting drunk during Oktoberfest and fucking on the floor of some hostel in France. Sometimes I think about how they ran out of money over there and how they started stealing food to get by, and I think of us holding up shops and I wonder whether it takes Andy back. Sometimes I think about my hair and how it's the same colour as hers and I think about how safe she makes him feel, and

---

sometimes I wonder if they would still be together if Kiran didn't hate relationships so much. Sometimes I think that I'm just a replacement.

The next morning, when I walk past on the way to the showers, James is sitting outside his trailer with his guitar between his legs, fiddling with the strings.

Inside the toilet block, I put my towel on the rack in the little hallway and strip. There aren't any cubicles. It's just a tiled room with a bunch of shower-heads that spray stinging, glacial-cold water and a couple of drains that are routinely clogged with hair.

Kiran is washing herself when I enter the room.

She's got her back to me, which is covered in dragon ink, and she's scrubbing under her arms. I watch the water run between her shoulder blades, down her spine, and over her ass.

James bought his trailer from an old carny he once knew. It's painted a deep green colour which is licked red with some-thing that's supposed to look like fire, and maybe did once, and there's sharp stalagmite lettering that reads, 'Satan Spawn.' It's dulled now, muddy looking, and the finish is chipped. It's evening when I go over there, and I notice that one of the strands of fairy lights wrapped around his window is dead. I can hear him playing guitar.

I knock on the door. The guitar playing stops.

The door opens and James is standing there in a vest and his underpants. 'Chantelle?'

'Can I come in?'

James doesn't say anything. He looks me up and down, lingering on my tits and the denim shorts I'm wearing, and rubs his chin. He looks out into the dark, as if to judge whether he's being watched, and then steps backs and holds the door open for me.

'Sure.'

The inside of the trailer stinks of moonshine. It's bare except for a tatty armchair, a cooker, stacks of vinyl records, and a rifle that is mounted on the wall. 'Sorry for the smell.' He indicates the bucket that sits in the corner of the floor, with rubber bands holding the cheese cloth over its top. 'It tickles some girls the wrong way.'

'Not me.'

'No?' He walks over to the kitchen side and pours two glasses of whiskey. 'Then you must be one of those other type of girls.' He hands me a glass, making a point of stroking my hand with the tips of his long fingers.

I take a drink. 'Maybe I am.'

'Maybe.'

Then, not knowing exactly where to go from here, I lean close and kiss him on the lips. Our legs are touching and I feel his hairs bristling against my shins. He pulls back, looks at me, then grabs my ass and forces me toward him. I kiss him again, and then again, using tongue, his stubble prickly against my face. I run my palm up and down his chest and dip into his underpants and start rubbing his balls, feeling him go hard along my forearm. Then he grabs me and takes me to the bed and I pull his vest off him and when he fucks me, I claw his chest and make sure to scream.

The next morning Andy makes coffee.

'What did you get up to last night?' he asks.

'Went for a run,' I tell him, not looking up from Rolling Stone. Some article about Prince's new band.

'Really? All night?'

'Yeah.'

'Okay, okay,' he says, nodding. We lock eyes and in that moment I know that he heard me and he knows that I know that. He walks over and puts a mug down on the fold-out table in front of me.

'Here, coffee.'

We leave the scrubland shortly after that. The IDs Kiran was sorting out for us arrive, though I have a suspicion that Andy had them all along. I had wanted my new name to be Jess, but for some reason my new passport calls me Alice Whittaker, which is okay I guess. Andy is now Phillip Greenberg, which sounds a bit too Jewish, but he says it'll do. Kiran dyes my hair blue in her sink and pierces my nose and eyebrow in her living room. I ask whether she thinks it'll get infected and she says that she doesn't think so and when I ask how she knows this she shrugs and says she doesn't.

Andy shaves his head, bald.

Kiran drives us into the nearest town and leaves us in the parking lot outside Walmart. 'Good luck,' she says, giving Andy a kiss. She turns to me and wraps her arms around my waist, crushing me a little. 'And you,' she says. 'You take care of yourself.'

I tell her that I will, and I'm surprised how hard it seems for her to let go. Maybe she doesn't want me to breathe.

'This isn't a goodbye,' she says, 'I'll see you and Andy real soon, Christmas maybe.' She goes on and on like that, and all I want her to do is get in her pick-up and leave.

Dorothy

Olga Dermott-Bond

Greasy rain smeared and squeaked across the windscreen, as the engine coughed slowly to a strained silence. Almost immediately, the cold slid underneath the car door, like someone else's unwanted phantom cat, interrupting an artificial warmth, a fuggy mottled smell. Dorothy's hands (which had never been beautiful) rested swollen on the steering wheel, a patchwork of veins and liver spots.

The empty car park looked strange this time of night. The white lines took on a strange meaning, like a fool's alphabet. It would get even colder later. She would have to get the blanket and flask out of the boot.

Every little helps.

In her rear view mirror, the supermarket still glared, an ugly modern Cathedral. She had known Derek didn't love her. -he notion that he might have been eaten up and thrown away years ago. *Indifference*. That's the word, Dorothy thought. It had shrink-wrapped her whole life. Down the aisles of memory everything seemed harshly lit, out of reach. She didn't want any of it.

A solitary rat ambled towards the blue industrial bins.

Devotion. That was the word that made her hands tighten on the wheel. As if, when her mother had corseted her into wedding dress thirty two years ago, she had inserted a long-life battery of aiming to please.

For Better?

There hadn't been much of that. For Worse. Worse. Worse.

She had been coming here for the past three weeks. Always parked in the same spot. Such choice at this time of night. Not like normal; neck tense, time watching, trolley grabbing, always something forgotten off the list.

Dorothy reached round her seat awkwardly into the back for her extra cardi. Brought it for every grocery trip. She was always bewildered by the skinny young mums in their strappy tops reaching into the freezers for the chicken nuggets.

Outside, two empty crisp packets were being pummelled with the rain, lying lopsided like unconvincing lies. The picture of night grew blurred once more.

Three weeks ago, she had found it. In the kitchen bin, that is. She had taken it out. Unopened. The birthday card she had chosen for Derek on one of her shopping trips. Dorothy had felt it happen - the acid leaking out of the battery that had kept her spinning with the promise that she might, some day, get something back in return.

Dissection. That word brought a smile to her lips. She had excavated his body like an ancient Roman Town, looking for any remnant of his humanity. Most of him was still in the freezer. Last week it had been his testicles. Dorothy had sat for nearly three hours and watched the rats feast.

The rain showed no sign of stopping. Her hair would have to get wet, frizz and go brittle. With a sigh, Dorothy heaved her cardigan on, and squelched in her slippers over to the blue bins. In her 'Bag for Life' was Derek's left hand, the wedding ring still awkwardly embedded in the defrosting flesh.

Every December Sky

Les Wood

It was one of those days when the light in the sky gave Kyle the strange feeling that he had lived before. An intangible sense in the back of his mind, like the foggy limbo felt on the cusp of coming awake after falling asleep in the middle of the afternoon. Nothing he could grasp with any certainty, just a feeling... almost, but not quite, a memory that he'd had a previous life.

It was not an unusual feeling for Kyle - a smell or a song could trigger it, or a sound or a taste, but most often it was the dimming of the light on a day like this: getting towards dusk, low, dark clouds the colour of a winter sea, heavy with the threat of snow and, far on the horizon, a weak, watery sun filtering through the bleak greyness to cast a dim yellow glow on the Glasgow streets. Whatever caused it, it was as if the universe tilted on its axis for a moment and he felt himself struggling to grasp at memories he wasn't entirely sure were there at all.

Of course, he never mentioned any of this to anyone, least of all his mates. They wouldn't understand, think him an A-number-one candidate for the loony bin. What the fuck was he talking about? Was he off his trolley? But Kyle wondered if there were times when they shared the same thoughts and feelings. That maybe everyone had a trigger, a sequence of events, a coincidence of circumstances, that awoke a deep, latent memory, but, like him, they kept quiet about it.

Perhaps he attached too much importance to it, after all it was just a feeling and, if he was to be honest about it, he didn't believe all this Buddhist-style shite meant anything.

Kyle parked his car in a side street and started to walk the couple of blocks down to The Palace. To park outside would just make it obvious to any nosy bastard who cared to look that there was something going on in the derelict bingo hall. Christ only knew why Boddice had picked this spot for the meet. The hall was due for demolition in a couple of weeks. Safe enough, Kyle supposed, for whatever Boddice had in mind. Boddice always liked to have some sort of security for these things, especially if he was arranging a hit. He could have been a bit more informative with his text message though – Boddice at the Palace, 4.00. It had taken Kyle a minute or two to work out where and what the fuck the Palace was.

The sun finally disappeared behind the tower blocks in the distance and a squally wind threw sleety rain in his face. Kyle pulled his jacket closer around him and ran his hand through his hair. It needed cut – he'd have to get Mary to go over it with the clippers. Number 3 all over. Boddice wouldn't allow them to have it any shorter, said it attracted unwanted attention. From wee neds wanting to have a go to see if you were as hard as you looked, to the polis cruising for someone who looked as if they needed to be flung in the back of the car. True, the shorter it was, the more aggressive and intimidating you looked (usually - Kyle thought it made some guys look like overgrown babies) but Boddice didn't want overt aggression. People knew what to expect if they saw that. Much better to go in with the softer look and then surprise them when things didn't turn out quite as they anticipated.

Whatever … he would get Mary to see to it later tonight. He was in danger of turning into a hippy. He smiled. Maybe that was what was behind all this previous-life crap. He'd get his hair cut and return, like a reversal of Samson, to normality.

He arrived at the Palace. Loose plaster hung down from the awning over the front doors and the black plastic letters B N G clung to their little attachment rails on the overhead marquee like the final notes in a musical score. A faded day-glo poster announced the appearance of Les Dennis on the fifth of March. What the fuck year must that have been?

Kyle noticed Leggett's car parked directly outside; a souped-up Corsa, bright red with rear spoiler. The wee turd never stopped to think, did he?

The front entrance was boarded and shuttered, and cast iron sliding gates were drawn across the stairs leading to the doors. Mounds of rubbish piled up behind the rails in scummy drifts. Kyle moved round to the side of the building, clambering through the overgrown weeds and mud-sludged puddles, and found the fire exit. The door was banging back and forth in the wind. He grabbed it and pulled it open, wedging it in place with a wooden board crusted with cement. Standing in the doorway, he looked up the stair well that led to a dim flickering glow in the darkness above. He scrambled over a tarpaulin blocking the passageway and started up the stairs towards the light. At the top, he pushed open the swing doors, revealing the ruined carcass of the auditorium, and made his way towards the centre of the hall.

The Palace had at one time been a cinema and the seats that had once marched in rows of red-veloured splendour now lay scattered and broken amongst the rubble on the floor. Graffiti was sprayed on the walls, and someone had taken the trouble to draw a fairly impressive pornographic scene on the side of the staircase leading to the broken stage. Flurries of snowflakes drifted down from a hole in the roof and the matted carpet squelched under his feet as he walked across to the small fire that one of the guys had started in the middle of the floor.

It looked as if he was the last one to arrive. The Wilson twins stood off to one side smoking, coats buttoned and collars turned up against the cold. Prentice sat on the edge of the stage, staring glumly at the dark recesses of the balcony, the light from the fire flickering in his eyes. Boag sat on his hunkers, warming his hands at the flames, his face drawn and pale. As Kyle approached, Boag glanced up and looked away quickly. Kyle hadn't seen him for a while and he wondered if he was sleeping rough. The thought crossed his mind to maybe lend him a wee bung when they were through with this. He gave Boag a nod and half a smile as he walked up to join him at the fire.

No-one spoke - except for the boy Leggett. He just wouldn't shut the fuck up.

'Wee-hoo!' he yipped to no-one in particular, kicking up a pile of yellowed bingo cards and clapping his hands excitedly. 'Oh man, oh man! Ah think this might be it. Ah think big Boddice is gonnae pick me this time! What do youse think guys?'

No-one paid him any attention. None of the others really liked him that much. Too much of a liability on whatever jobs he'd been trusted to take part in. Too much of a loose cannon. Too much of a fuckwit. Kyle put his hands in his pockets and stared into the fire.

'Oh aye,' Leggett went on. 'Youse've all done this kind of thing before, Ah know. Ah think it's gonnae be my turn now, but. Ah've been practising too…' Kyle lifted his head and looked over at him, '… using dugs and cats and that, and Ah know my wee air pistol isn't quite the same thing, but it does the business, ye know?' Leggett picked up a piece of plastic tubing from the floor and hurled it to the back of the hall where it clattered behind a balustrade decorated with little silver and gold crowns. 'The wee fuckers sometimes get away, but most-times Ah get them clean. Pow! Right in the eye or the balls!' He spun round, cocking his thumb back and making a pistol of his hand. 'Wee-hoo! Ye should see them. They just fold up, all yelpin and whinin. Fuckin magic! And then Ah'll go over and step on their necks or their ribs till they stop.' He sniggered and shook his head. "Aye. Ah think he's gonnae give me my chance, big Boddice.' He clasped his hands and straightened both arms in front of him, screwing up his eyes and taking aim along the length of his arm towards his thumb. 'Pow!'

Kyle stared at him and spat on the floor.

Leggett turned his head. 'What's your fuckin problem, Kyle?' Leggett said, lifting his chin, curling his lip at him.

The twins turned to look at him. The others didn't move,

couldn't be arsed.

Leggett folded his arms, took up a defiant stance. 'You not think Ah've got it in me? Eh, Kyle? You got a problem?'

You're fucking right I've got a problem, Kyle thought. He was about to say something, about to walk over and wipe that stupid sneer off Leggett's face, when there was a sudden rushing of wind in the hall and the snowflakes falling from the roof swirled and danced above the flames of the fire. The door at the back of the hall opened and there was McLean, Boddice's right hand man, his minder, his trusted lieutenant, striding down the aisle towards them.

McLean was a big man, tall and hefty, with his hair oiled and swept back and his greying beard neatly trimmed. He wore a long, dark overcoat with a yellow cashmere scarf tucked neatly around his neck. Black leather gloves covered his hands and the scent of expensive aftershave drifted towards the men as he approached. Leggett was looking at him expectantly, his hands fidgeting with the buttons on his jacket.

'All right, boys?' said McLean. 'Glad you could make it.'

'Ah'm just fine, Mr. McLean,' said Leggett, not realising the question didn't require an answer. 'Just fine.'

McLean didn't even look at him. 'Mr. Boddice apologises - he has been unavoidably detained,' he said. 'But he will be glad to learn you all received his message and took the trouble to come out on this foul night to attend to business.' He reached into his coat and took out a bundle wrapped in a dark blue towel. McLean unfolded the package slowly to reveal a snub-nosed revolver, chrome plated. It lay gleaming on the towel, reflecting the flames from the fire. He placed it carefully on the floor.

'Holy mother of all things holy,' said Leggett in a hushed voice. 'Fuck me, but that's a beauty! Sheee-ite! Can Ah touch it?'

McLean turned his head slightly and raised an eyebrow. 'Don't be so fucking stupid!' he snapped. 'Mr. Boddice paid over eight hundred for this weapon. Imported from Holland. Never fired.' He looked at each of them in turn. 'There's one bullet and then it goes back tomorrow. It'll be untraceable.' He turned to Leggett. 'So Ah don't want your grubby wee mitts on it alright?'

Leggett looked dejected.

'Not yet anyway.' McLean finished.

Leggett's eyes widened, and a grin spread across his face. He hopped from foot to foot. 'Oh man, oh man,' he muttered under his breath.

'Okay boys,' said McLean. 'Sorry this has been a wee hike for most of youse. Mr. Boddice hopes you will forgive him. But it's a single shot job. Ah don't need youse all for this one.'

They had heard all this before. Boddice always liked to have his full team at his disposal and usually didn't make up his mind who he would use on a particular job until the last minute. A wee text message on the mobile, giving the time and place for the meet, and he'd expect them all to be there. Failure to show and they'd never be used again. Simple as that. He'd make sure each of them got a wee something for their trouble, but it was never that much. Nevertheless, if any of them was picked for one of the "special" jobs, the rewards were handsome; and that's what kept them coming back.

McLean stood for a moment in silence, contemplating. He closed his eyes and took a deep breath. 'Leggett, it's you,' he said eventually.

Leggett let out a wee gasp. 'Oh fuckin mama… yes!' he said.

McLean went on. 'And Kyle, Ah'll need you as well.'

Kyle's heart skipped a beat or two. He glanced over at Leggett who was still too excited to notice what McLean had said. Oh fuck, thought Kyle. I think I know what's coming.

McLean ushered the rest of them from the hall. 'Right lads. See the rest of youse next time. Let yourselves out the back.'

The others filed out through the back of the hall and Kyle noticed that McLean held Boag back for a minute, exchanged a few low words with him and slipped a couple of twenties into his coat pocket.

All the time Leggett was eyeing the gun lying glistening on the towel. It shone in the darkness like a bead of mercury. He licked his lips and looked up at Kyle, seeming to notice for the first time that he was still there, that they were a twosome and that Leggett wasn't in this one on his own. A small frown creased his forehead.

McLean came back down the aisle towards the fire, bent down and picked up the gun, holding it carefully in the towel, despite his gloved hands. Leggett shifted back and forth restlessly, barely able to contain himself, his eyes darting between McLean and the gun.

'Kyle,' McLean said, turning towards him. 'You've done this for Mr. Boddice before, haven't ye?'

Kyle nodded.

He felt the universe tilt on its axis.

McLean came over and handed the gun to Kyle. 'Okay, do him,' he said, and walked quickly to the doors at the back of the hall.

Kyle turned to Leggett who was looking at him with innocent, uncomprehending eyes. Eyes like those in the animals he'd shot. Eyes that were growing wider by the second as he slowly realised what was about to happen. Leggett started gibbering; senseless fractured phrases. 'No, it's alright… Ah don't need to know… Ah'm a good boy…'

Kyle became aware of the banging of the fire exit door down in the depths of the building. It must have worked its way free of the board propping it open.

The sound reminded him of something. He couldn't quite place it.

He levelled the gun and squeezed the trigger.

Pow!

Classic Romantics

Molly Miltenberger Murray

'I come here the minute I hear the ripple of the Adagio. I can't resist hands crashing down the octaves, coming down the keys like waves.

That's how I met Martin. We were at the symphony. He said that when he saw me a few rows down, he couldn't take his eyes off of me. I seemed to be so sensitive to the music.

He told me this when he brought me a glass of red wine during intermission. Before he tasted his, he swirled his glass to savor the essence, watching the deep red legs trickling down the bowl. *Would you join me for dinner?* He asked.

Over a white candle at my favorite Mediterranean we shared our favorite music, our secret guilty pleasures. He was scared to tell; I pushed him. The blood rushed to his face while he said it.

Victrolas. He said it with a start. He could not resist a classic Victrola. Each individual instrument is marked by idiosyncrasies. The machine's voice is distinct like the interpretation of a pianist. The same song on the same record will sound completely different on two different Victrolas because they carry this individual signature. *You are so sensitive to voice and interpretation; you would be enthralled.*

He invited me to come in to see his collection.

I didn't.

No.

Not until our third date. We sat right here where you and I are sitting now. He popped the bottle and poured me a glass. *To all of us classic romantics!* he said. I said, *Hear, hear.* Our glasses met. They chimed like crystal.

He stood up then, to open his prize Victrola. *Call me old-school*, he said. *But I love the sound of a real record. I'm crazy about the breaks, the cracks, the experience of emotion.* I raised my glass.

Then he slipped on the Beethoven and set the stylus. The notes grew; a performance; too loudly to hear myself think. I listened to the white space for a minute 'til I heard the signature, and nodded to show my appreciation.

I leaned over to his ear. *Could you turn it down?* He said he could not: this passage was very important to the performance. I felt his hands rippling up my back. I let myself become immersed in the sonata. Music washed over me like waves while his hands surged across my back.

Pressure.

Glorious intensity, growing with music I experienced like I never experienced before. Fingers pulled off my shift and my leggings. I felt it in my bones, felt it within my core.

Raw, naked, listening.

Adagio. Allegretto. Presto.

Oscillations.

Percussions.

Tingling, vellicating, convulsing.

Thrusting.

Compressing.

Breaking.

Billows of music enveloped my screams. Surges of pain pinned me to the sofa. This sofa. The music grasped a climax. Martin grappled my neck. Strangling.

Severing. The song ended with my breath.'

The little ghost faded into the corners of the sofa as *Moonlight Sonata* closed. The Victrola still whispered. A key turned in the lock. Martin, back with the wine.

Sadie didn't know what to do.

Making Mr Harper Happy

Eddie Bell

'No, pull it this way so it's hanging out of the side.'

Graham heaved, doing as he was told. This time they had outdone themselves. Mr Harper would be so proud. *Harper's Haunted tours* would no doubt be the number one tourist attraction in the City now. Graham was sure of it.

Receiving further instructions from Brian, who saw himself as the boss, Graham tied the laces in a double bow. They didn't want to leave anything to chance. Once secure, he took a step backwards and gulped down a swig from a bottle of water that rested on the side.

'You sure Mr Harper would approve of this?' Graham asked his co-worker who was standing admiring their work alongside him.

'Of course. We need to improve revenue is what he said. To do that, we need to advertise, and by that, he didn't mean just to hand out rubbish little leaflets that only get chucked in the bin.'

'I guess it will attract attention.'

'Exactly,' Brian said, patting Graham hard on his back causing him to wince. 'Now come on, let's finish off so we can get out onto the streets and pull in the punters.'

For the next hour, Graham and Brian worked solidly, barely talking, unless it was to give and receive further instructions. It was hard work and the conditions weren't the best with various smells seeping into their nostrils and the freezing temperature leaking in from outside. But eventually they were finished.

'This is amazing,' Brian beamed with delight. Graham had to agree. It certainly caught the eye and the sign looked good erected from the handles of the apple cart, telling people to catch the tour at 8pm from outside the Black Swan pub.

'Ready?' Brian asked.

Graham nodded his head and lifted the handle on the cart.

'Bloody hell, it's heavy,' he moaned, using all his muscle to hold the cart steady.

They made it out onto the busy streets, tourists taking great interest as Brian shouted at the top of his voice. Graham struggled to direct the cart in the direction he wanted it to go, almost crashing a couple of times. Finally he got the hang of it and they spent hours walking, racking up bookings for that evening's tour.

Only when their legs and Graham's arms wouldn't take it anymore, did the pair return to their shed. Relishing taking the weight off his arms, Graham and Brian shared a high-five and sat down for a well-deserved break.

'You think he would have been happy with that then?' Graham asked.

Brian got up and walked over to the creation that had attracted so much attention. Prising a plaque from Mr Harper's hands, he read aloud: 'Telling the scariest tales from beyond the grave.'

'Oh aye, Mr Harper will be *dead* happy,' he said as he patted the corpse of their boss on the head.

Biographies

Eddie Bell has been writing stories for the past couple of years; this is his first submission. After many attempts and many half-finished stories, he is currently in the middle of writing a novel based around the suspected murder of a man and the disappearance of his wife.

Nichola Deadman was born in South Africa. She studied Political Science at the University of Pretoria before moving to Japan to teach English. She is currently enrolled in the University of Glasgow's MLitt Creative Writing programme. She enjoys crochet, cooking, and reminiscing about when she had time to do either.

Olga Dermott-Bond is a teacher of English and Drama. Originally from Northern Ireland, she studied English Literature at St. Andrews University. She now lives in Warwickshire with her husband and two young daughters. She was Warwick Poet Laureate in 2010, and enjoys all kinds of creative writing.

morgan downie writes poems and short stories. Though not unacquainted with violence he lives a peaceful life. He considers the niche of fashion based slasher poetry his alone.

Max Dunbar was born in London in 1981. He recently finished a full-length novel and his short fiction and criticism has appeared in various print and web journals. He blogs at http://maxdunbar.wordpress.com/ and tweets at http://twitter.com/MaxDunbar1. Max Dunbar lives in Leeds and can be contacted on max.dunbar@gmail.com.

Sleiman El Hajj has studied creative writing at Exeter College, Oxford University, and is a doctoral candidate in creative writing at the University of Gloucestershire, UK. Sleiman obtained his MA in English literature from the American University of Beirut where he also studied biology and American Studies. His current research explores—in and through creative narrative—constructions of home in post-post-war (post-2006) Lebanon in relation to green spaces, queers, Lebanese women, female migrant workers, and refugees. Sleiman's creative and critical writings have appeared in *Excursions Journal*, *Prole: Poetry and Prose Magazine*, and in *Carnival: New Writing III Anthology*.

J. David Jaggers lives in fly-over country where he spends his days in the white collar world and his nights feeding the thugs, pimps and enforcers he keeps caged in his basement. He has been published in the usual places, including *Near to the Knuckle*, *Yellow Mama*, *Spelk* and *Out of the Gutter* magazines.

For many years **Sue Iles-Jonas** was a criminologist working for the criminal justice system. Although she has now left the dark side and is a clinical hypnotherapist she finds time to write crime fiction in the form of short stories and she is just doing the final edit on her first novel '*A Bunch of Lies.*'
She is a member of West Sussex Writers and has found some success with her comedy noir combo in Sussex open mics and club competitions. Her second novel will be a tale of female revenge.

Wendy H. Jones lives in, Scotland, and her police procedural series featuring Detective Inspector Shona McKenzie, is set in the beautiful city of Dundee, Scotland. Wendy has led a varied and adventurous life. Her love for adventure led to her joining the Royal Navy to undertake nurse training. After six years in the Navy she joined the Army where she served as an Officer for a further 17 years. This took her all over the world including Europe, the Middle East and the Far East. Much of her spare time is now spent travelling around the UK, and lands much further afield. As well as nursing Wendy also worked for many years in Academia. This led to publication in academic textbooks and journals. *Killer's Countdown* is her first novel and the first book in the Shona McKenzie Mystery series.

B. D. Lamont is an MLitt Creative Writing student at Glasgow University. Her work has recently been included in the University's publication, *From Glasgow To Saturn*. She mainly writes horror fiction.

Alyson Lawson is a teacher somewhere near sunny Glasgow. She spends her time marking essays, telling kids that, "NO Shakespeare isn't still alive", "Orwell invented Big Brother not Channel 4 ...or Channel 5" and correcting youngsters who think Charles Dickens wrote Anne Frank's Diary. Oh, and occasionally attempting to be a writer.

Reece McCormack is a 20-year-old undergraduate, studying Creative Writing at the University of Gloucestershire.

Kerrie McKinnel is a mum and a creative writing student at the University of Glasgow. Between dealing with toddler tantrums and one-word-a-page board books, she enjoys reading, walking and baking. Her fiction writing is inspired by her experiences of motherhood, and the occasional fleeting memory of what life used to be like when her home was quiet and did not smell like nappies and milk. She lives in Scotland with her husband and son.

David McVey teaches Communication at New College Lanarkshire. He has published over 100 short stories and a great deal of non-fiction that focuses on history and the outdoors. He enjoys hillwalking, visiting historic sites, reading, watching telly, and supporting his home-town football team, Kirkintilloch Rob Roy FC.

At various times in his life, **Christopher P. Mooney** has been a supermarket cashier, a shelf stacker, a barman, a cinema usher, a carpet-fitter's labourer, a foreign-language assistant and, for the past twelve years, a secondary-school teacher. He enjoys teaching but would rather be a writer. He was born and grew up in Glasgow and spent two years living in France. In addition to short crime fiction, he also writes bad poetry and is working on his first novel. He currently lives in a small house near London with his wife and two children.

Helen Morris lives and works in Essex. She has just started writing short stories. She is on twitter @mortaltaste if anyone wants to say hello.

Sarah Palmer is studying for an MLitt with the University of Glasgow creative writing programme.

Katy Simmonds doesn't remember making a conscious decision to write crime stories, but since *Hannah* is her second to be published, it seems to be happening anyway. Katy lived in Manchester for five years while studying at MMU and since completing her MA in Writing for Children, she has been writing and editing her first novel for Young Adults and plotting her return to Manchester.

David Warde had a full career in the British Army, and came to writing late in life. He lives in Scotland with his wife Carol and their two sons, Ruairidh (pronounced Rory) and Cameron (pronounced Cameron!). David's other interests include making bespoke presents from such diverse materials as camel-bone, buffalo horn, deer-antler, wood and silver.

10619082R00071

Printed in Great Britain
by Amazon.co.uk, Ltd.,
Marston Gate.